THE

CARD BOOK

*Interactive Games
and Activities
for Language Learners*

**Abigail Tom
Heather McKay**

Alta Book Center Publishers—San Francisco

14 Adrian Court, Burlingame, California 94010 USA

Illustrations: Manuel F. Cheo
Cover Design: Leigh McLellan
Editor: John Duffy
Original Copyright ©1991 by Prentice-Hall Regents

© 2000 Alta Book Center Publishers—San Francisco
14 Adrian Court
Burlingame, California 94010 USA

Phone: 800 ALTA/ESL I 650.692.1285
Fax: 800 ALTA/FAX I 650.692.4654
Email: info@altaesl.com I www.altaesl.com

Printed in the United States of America

ISBN 1-882483-79-0

CONTENTS

CARD SETS

Clothing ✧

Shirts
Jeans
Skirt
Woman's bathing suit
Slacks
Shorts
Sweater
Coat
Winter jacket
Sandals
High-heeled shoes
Running shoes
Man's oxfords
Tuxedo
Suit
Necktie
T-shirt
Man's bathing suit
Socks
Gloves
Wristwatch
Bathrobe
Pajamas
Sportcoat
Chain/necklace
Ring
Belt

Food ✿

Apple
Orange
Banana
Cup of coffee
Bowl of soup
Bread
Chicken
Steak
Hamburger
Carrot
Potato
Lemon
Onion
Eggs
Milk
Spaghetti
Ice cream cone
Pizza
Strawberry
Grapes
Rice
Chocolate cake
Apple pie
Lettuce
Corn
Fish
Green pepper

Furniture ✳

Sofa
Armchair
End table
Coffee table
Desk
Floor lamp
Television set
Bookcase
Telephone
Sink
Stove
Refrigerator
Toilet
Bathtub
Bathroom sink
Bed
Dresser
Kitchen table
Straight chair
Cupboard
Dishwasher
Microwave oven
Stereo
Chest of drawers
Mirror
Table lamp
Washing machine

Animals ✿	Road Signs ✣	Tools ✴
Snake	Stop	Hammer
Whale	Curve	Screwdriver
Fish	Merge	Crowbar
Fly	No Entry	Nails
Bird	Picnic Table	Screws
Horse	Hill	Saw
Cow	No Parking	Pliers
Pig	No Left Turn	Needle
Lobster	Men Working	Thread
Dog	No Right Turn	Oil can
Cat	Lane Ends	Scissors
Ant	School Crossing	Coat hanger
Chicken	Railroad Crossing	Corkscrew
Turtle	Deer Crossing	Jackknife
Tiger	Camping	Pencil
Butterfly	Food	Paint brush
Zebra	Telephone	Paper clip
Cockroach	Winding Road	Can opener
Mouse	Snowmobile	Key
Sheep	Cattle Crossing	Rope
Elephant	No Trucks	Electric drill
Duck	Slippery When Wet	Spoon
Giraffe	55 MPH	Fork
Owl	Lodging	Shovel
Rabbit	Airport	Ruler
Shark	Gas Station	File
Monkey	Restrooms	Magnifying glass

Faces ▽

Tops of faces (hair, foreheads)
Middles of faces (eyes, noses, ears, hair)
Bottoms of faces (chins, mouths)

Daily Activities

Turn off alarm
Wake up
Exercise
Take a shower
Shave
Put on makeup
Get dressed
Comb hair
Cook
Eat
Brush teeth
Leave house
Catch bus
Work
Go to supermarket
Watch television
Read paper
Wash face
Drive car
Lock door
Open window
Turn on light
Drink coffee
Sweep
Wash clothes
Iron
Wash dishes

Leisure Activities ☆

Ski
Read a book
Play the guitar
Play baseball
Play soccer
Play basketball
Have a picnic
Surf
Play ping-pong
Ride a bicycle
Go for a drive
Talk with friends
Listen to music
Go to a movie
Play tennis
Fish
Climb a mountain
Dance
Swim
Sit on a beach
Ice skate
Run
Fly a kite
Sail
Paint a picture
Go camping
Go sledding

ACKNOWLEDGMENTS

Changing Faces. The original idea for this activity comes from a children's game called "Change a Face," which comes complete with a special box and face masks. "Change a Face" made minimal use of language but served as a starting point for the activity. Contact Makor Games, Israel.

It's All in the Face. The activity of making up questions about faces can be found in several places. One very good version is in an article by Penny Ur, "Flashcards for Groupwork," in *Modern English Teacher*, Volume 8, No. 1 (1980).

What Will You Do With It? is a fairly well known activity. A version was suggested by Glenys Hanson in "Ideas for Picture Flashcard Games," in *Modern English Teacher*, Volume 8, No. 1.

Describe and Draw and *Describe and Arrange* are well-known activities. They appear in the 1979 *ELT Guide: Communication Games* by Don Byrne and Shelagh Rixon.

By the same authors: *Writing Warm Ups* (1999), Alta Book Center Publishers; *Eureka! Science Demonstrations for ESL Classes* (1999), Alta Book Center Publishers; *Teaching Adult Second Language Learners* (1999), Cambridge University Press.

NOTES TO THE TEACHER

Using This Book

Welcome to *The Card Book*. We wrote it because we (and other teachers) wanted some basic pictures in an easy-to-use format. In this book we have provided nine sets of picture cards which we feel will be useful in a variety of classroom settings. The card sets include clothing, food, furniture, animals, road signs, tools, faces, daily activities and leisure activities. The twenty-seven pictures in each set are big enough to be easily seen but small enough to fit on a desktop and to use for games and small group activities. We made them reproducible so teachers can make copies for all of their students and replace them easily.

In the following section labeled "Generic Activities" you will find ways to introduce the cards and to practice them. These basic suggestions and activities can be used with all of the cards and are most appropriate for beginning students. In the remainder of the book, after each set of cards, we provide additional activities that require familiarity with the cards and are more suitable for high beginning and intermediate students. Within those sections we have distinguished three interactive activity types: information sharing, opinion sharing and problem solving. In the first, and generally easiest, category, information sharing, we include those activities in which the participants do not have the same information. They must get the missing information from each other in order to complete a task. This type of activity requires students to elicit information and ask clarifying questions. In the second group of activities, opinion sharing, students must find out each other's opinions in order to complete a task. In this type of activity, agreement and disagreement, clarification and explanation are expected. In the problem solving activities, pairs or groups of students are required to share information, suggestions and opinions and apply the results to the solution of the problem.

Interactive activities such as these are useful to students who will work or study in English as they enable the learners to practice the "glue" of social and academic interaction (those expressions which are commonly used when working and conversing with others). Certain interactive functions and their linguistic realizations are needed for the completion of these tasks. Because these functions underlie and are useful for all of the activities given, we have not listed them with each task. However, we have included a list of them for the teacher's use in Appendix A, "Language for Interaction" (p. 141). If desired, these functions can be specifically taught to students before they work with the activities.

We hope that as you use the cards, you will build on the basic vocabulary they provide and find ways to integrate them with other materials as you plan thematic units. Specific activities should be selected with reference to the curriculum and interests of the students. To help you with this, we have provided, in Appendix B and

Appendix C, lists of functions and grammatical structures that appear in specific activities. Appendix D gives a list of life skills covered in each section of the book.

In writing these activities we have made every effort to make them easy to use. Game boards and reproducible pages are provided. None of the activities require extensive pre-class preparation or special equipment.

Generic Activities

During the years since *The Card Book* was first published, we have had considerable experience working with the cards, both in our own classes and in teacher training workshops. When working with beginners we have often found ourselves returning to a basic set of activities not previously included in this book. It is these generic activities that we would like to share with you here. We have arranged them in order of increasing difficulty.

1. Cutting and Labeling

The first thing we realized about the cards is that, when preparing a set of cards for each student, the teacher does not have to cut and label a set for each student. Instead, you can hand out one page and some scissors and have the students cut them out. Then, for true beginners, you can go through the cards one by one, writing the word or words on the board and having the students label the back of each card. As the class completes one sheet of nine cards, they can practice them before going on to the next.

For higher level students, you can make and post a list of the labels, either sheet by sheet or for the whole set, and have the students work together to determine which words match which cards and to label them.

This whole process gives the students a sense of ownership of the cards which they don't get if they are given a set of already prepared ones (and, of course, it saves you a lot of work). Students can make or bring in envelopes to hold the cards and should be encouraged to take the cards home with them to practice. When new or previously absent students come to the class, classmates can help them cut, identify and label their sets of cards.

2. Listening and Identifying

When the students have cut and labeled their cards, the next step is to say the name of a card and have the students hold it up. By doing this, you can check to see if the students can identify the cards and the students who are uncertain can look around at their neighbors' cards to see if they are correct without feeling embarrassed. This step can be repeated on subsequent days as a review.

After the students have heard all the vocabulary and understood its meaning, hold up each card and ask the students to repeat the word or phrase, first together and then individually. Check and correct pronunciation. This step can be repeated as a quick review on subsequent days.

3. Review Game

This is a good "beginning of class" activity, especially if some students come late or if there are new students who need time to cut and label their own cards.

The rest of the students can play this game with little supervision. Group students in threes. Have one student take the role of teacher and quiz the other students by showing a card for them to name. The student who names it first puts it in a stack in front of him. The student with the most cards at the end wins. Each student in turn can take the role of teacher.

4. Spelling Dictation

Choose 5-10 cards at a time. Spell the words on the cards aloud and have students write them on a piece of paper. Then have them hold up and say the name of each card they have spelled. For higher level students, read the letters out of order (*o-g-d,* for example, for *dog)* and have the students write the letters, identify the item and spell it correctly.

5. List Dictation

Dictate a shopping list using food, clothing, tool or furniture cards, including a quantity, a descriptor and/or a price for each item. You can also dictate a list of daily activities and times or a list of leisure activities with months (*I wake up at seven* or *I swim in July).*

6. Classification

Ask students to divide or select cards by certain criteria: color, shape, common trait (sleeves for clothing, winter activities for leisure activities, liquids for foods), or other criteria (things I like/don't like, wear/don't wear, do/don't do, have/don't have). See the activity on page 119 for an example. Initially you can state the criteria, but later students may want to show cards they believe go together while the rest of the class tries to guess the criteria. A variation of this is to have pairs of students put together sets of three cards, in which two cards go together and one does not, according to the criteria the students have chosen. The rest of the class tries to identify the card that does not belong as well as the criteria being used.

7. Definitions

Read a definition or description of the item on a card and have the students show you the card (for example, using food cards, describe the item: *It is long and yellow,* or for road sign cards, give clues like *curve left).* More advanced students can make their own definitions. Act out or have students act out those that represent actions.

8. Describe and Arrange

Have the students make a grid on a piece of paper, with three horizontal rows and three vertical rows, as in the original format of the cards. Designate each square by number (1, 2, 3) or for more advanced students, by location (top right, bottom left). Say the name of one of the cards and where to put it. Have the students put it in that place. Continue until all nine places are filled. Students can, after some practice with this activity, give their own directions to each other. See page 74 for an example of this activity type.

9. Kim's Game

This may be played on the same grid as "Describe and Arrange" (previous page). Have the students work in pairs. Ask student A to select and place pictures on the grid. Next give student B a limited time to memorize the arrangement before the pictures and grid are taken away. Then ask student B to describe the arrangement in as much detail as possible from memory. Finally, the students look at the original arrangement again to see if anything is missing or misplaced.

10. Concentration

Each group of three or four students will need a set of cards and a set of small strips with the names of the items on the cards. The cards and strips are put out on the table, upside down. Each student in turn, turns over a card and a strip and shows them to his group. If they match, he keeps them, if not, he puts them back. Everyone in the group tries to remember where each card and each strip is so that he can find a match when his turn comes. This game is best played on a dark surface so that the writing and pictures do not show through the paper.

11. Twenty Questions

Choose any card as a mystery object or activity. Conceal the card in some way and have the students ask yes/no questions to find out what the object or activity is. In a lower level class, the students may simply guess the object (*Is it a chair?*). Higher level students may be encouraged to ask questions about the *object* (*Is it cold? Is it made from milk?*) or in the case of activities like sports, you might set the object in the context of the past or future to encourage use of other verb tenses.

12. Old Maid

Choose any set of cards and one card from any other set. Use two complete sets of the chosen cards and one of the extra card for each group of four students. Have one player deal the cards so that each player gets the same number. One of the players will get an extra card. Then tell the students to look for matching pairs in their hands and to put the cards face up in front of them, naming the cards (e.g., *two dogs*). Next, each player in turn requests a specific card from any other player in order to form additional pairs. If the person who is asked has the card, she must give it to the player who asked for it. If not, she may give him any other card. If the first player gets the requested card, he puts down the resulting pair and names it. Play continues until all pairs have been formed and one person is left with the single card (this person is the "old maid"). A more advanced version is to have each player request a card by describing rather than naming the desired card.

We hope that these activities will provide you with a good starting point for using the cards and that you will enjoy using them as much as we do.

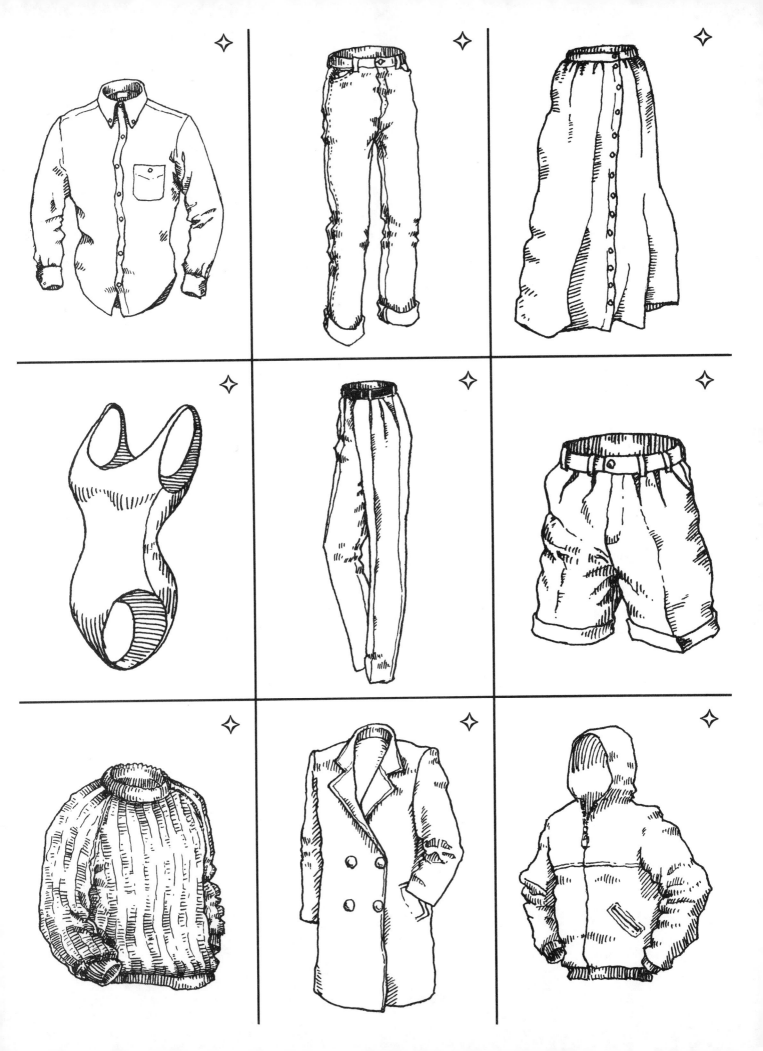

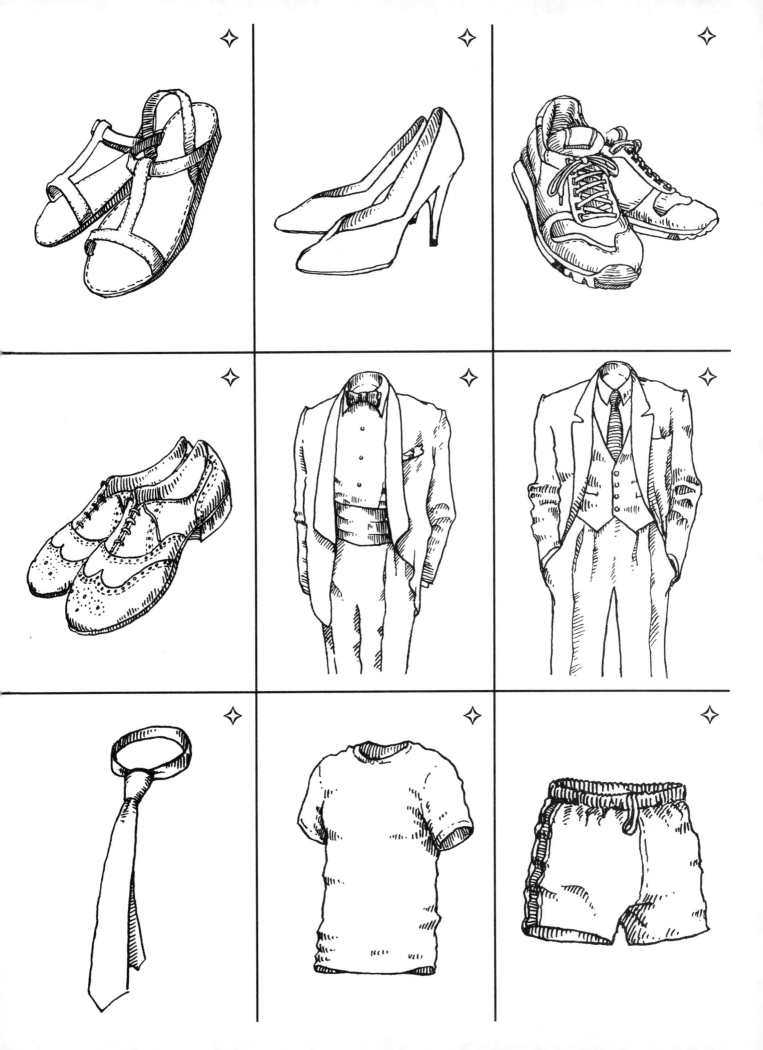

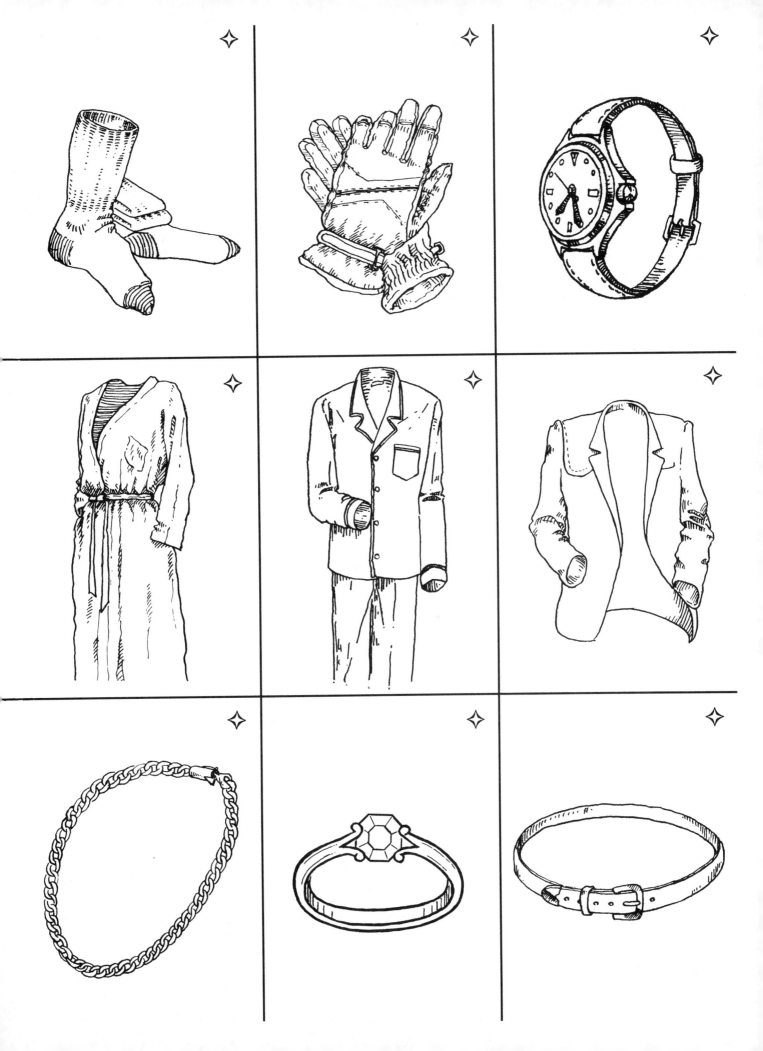

Buying and Selling

Task: To "buy" and "sell" items of clothing.

Materials: Three complete sets of Clothing Cards. Copy one set of cards on red paper. (These will be the *buying cards*.) Copy the other two sets of cards on blue paper. (These will be the *selling cards*.)

Procedure: Give each student one buying card and two selling cards. Explain to the students that they must try to "buy" the item shown on their buying card and "sell" the items on their selling cards.

Before beginning, ask students to write a price in pencil at the bottom of each card. The price indicates how much they are willing to pay for the item they must buy, and how much they are asking for the item they must sell.

Next, have all students walk around the room trying to buy and sell their items to other students in the class. Since there will be two sellers for each item, students must bargain to get the best prices. As they bargain, students may have to change the prices they have written on their cards. Students who have not sold their items may later auction them to the whole class.

A Shopping Trip

Task: To "buy" five items of clothing for less than $100.

Materials: Clothing advertisements from a variety of stores or mail order com-
             panies (Sears, K Mart, local stores, etc.). Enough Clothing Cards so
             that half the class will have five cards each, omitting cards for which
             advertisements cannot be found.

Procedure: Designate half the class as "buyers" and half as "sellers." Then,
             divide the sellers into groups of two or three students.

             Distribute the advertisements among the sellers. Ask them to look
             through their advertisements to get an idea of the cost of clothing—
             shoes, jackets, pants, etc. Seat the sellers in different locations
             around the classroom. Each group is a "classroom clothes shop."

             Now distribute five cards to each of the buyers. Tell them that they
             have a total of $100 to buy the five items on their cards. The buyers
             walk around the classroom, visiting the sellers' "classroom clothes
             shops." The buyers must learn where they can find the items they
             need and how much the items cost at each shop. The sellers try to
             persuade buyers to consider not only the price of an item but also the
             quality, color, and size selection. (For this information sellers can re-
             fer to their advertisements.)

             After buying an item, the buyer subtracts the cost from his $100. At
             the end of the activity, ask buyers and sellers to report on their expe-
             riences. Which sellers were most successful? Why? What did the stu-
             dents learn about staying within a budget? About price variations
             from store to store?

Variation: Have extra cards ready so that students can trade in one of their five
             cards and select another.

Clothes of the Rich and Famous

Task: To describe what famous people might wear. The object of the game is to match clothes with the famous people who might wear them.

Materials: One complete set of Clothing Cards and one die for each group of three or four students.

Procedure: Divide the class into groups of three or four students. Ask each group to choose six famous people, write down the names and number them. Suggest that the students' lists include men and women, older and younger people, and personalities in different fields, such as sports, politics, and entertainment.

Hand out one set of cards and one die to each group. The cards are placed face down in the middle of the group. The first player rolls the die. The number on the die indicates which famous person Player 1 will talk about.

After Player 1 has rolled the die, he or she picks up a card and makes a statement about the famous person and the clothes item on the card. For example, ''Queen Elizabeth never wears jeans'' or ''Michael Jackson wears only one glove.'' If the other players agree with the sentence, Player 1 gets the number of points shown on the die. If they disagree, Player 1 gets no points. After 15 to 20 minutes, the players add up their scores. The player with the most points is the winner.

Variation: If the class is diverse, not all students may be familiar with the same people. In that case, the teacher can provide each group with pictures of six different people. Students then play the game based on the pictures. Magazine advertisements are a good resource for this purpose.

1. Clothing Cards
   Opinion Sharing
   15–20 minutes

Guess Where I'm Going

Task: To guess where another person is going based on selected items of
            clothing.

Materials: One complete set of Clothing Cards for each group of three or four
            students.

Procedure: Divide the class into groups of three or four students and give each
            group a set of Clothing Cards.

            The cards are spread out face up in the middle of each group. One
            student thinks of a place he or she might go but doesn't tell the oth-
            ers. The student then chooses three items of clothing he or she would
            wear to this place. The rest of the group tries to guess where the stu-
            dent is going and what he or she will do there. The group may ask
            questions to get more information. The activity continues until each
            student has had two or three turns. (You may want to set a time limit
            on questions, say three or four minutes.)

Clothing Questions

Task: To answer questions about clothing.

Materials: One set of Clothing Cards, minus Wristwatch, Belt, and Ring cards.

Procedure: Have each student select a Clothing Card. Instruct students to listen carefully as the teacher (or another student) reads the Clothing Questions (below). Ask students to stand up if the item shown on their card answers the question.

As students stand up, have them tell the class which card they are holding. The other students decide if the answer is correct. In many cases, there is more than one answer. For the last two questions, students can explain why they would or would not wear the clothing items.

Clothing Questions

1. Who has something with a zipper?
2. Who has something with buttons?
3. Who has something that has sleeves?
4. Who has something that has a collar?
5. Who has something you can wear in the summer?
6. Who has something you can wear in the winter?
7. Who has something to wear on your feet?
8. Who has something to wear around your neck?
9. Who has something to wear to a formal party?
10. Who has something to wear to the beach?
11. Who has something you like to wear?
12. Who has something you would never wear?

Riddles

Task: To match riddles and Clothing Cards

Materials: Half the students in the class will each receive one of the following Clothing Cards: Shirt, Jeans, Winter jacket, Sandals, Running shoes, Tuxedo, Men's bathing suit, Socks, Gloves, Wristwatch, and Belt.

Students in the other half of the class will each receive one of 11 Riddle Strips (p. 13). (If the class is smaller than 22 students, use fewer strips and cards. If the class is larger, increase the number of cards and strips by using duplicates.)

Procedure: Write the following riddle on the board: *I wear you in the summer when the weather is hot. I wear you when I play tennis, but not when I go to work. I don't wear you in the winter because my knees would get cold.*

Ask the students to guess which item of clothing the riddle describes. Then have them tell you how they knew the riddle was about shorts.

Then give one Clothing Card each to half the students in the class. Give one Riddle Strip each to the remaining students. Ask all students to walk around the room until they find a match for their riddle or their card. Have all students share their answers when they finish. If there are disagreements, discuss them. This is a good way to divide students into pairs for another activity.

Variation: This activity can also be done entirely in pairs or small groups, with students matching all of the strips and cards.

Riddle Strips

There are buttons on your front and buttons on your sleeves.
There are even buttons on your collar.

After I wash you, I sometimes have trouble putting you on again
because you get smaller. But after I wear you for a while, you fit
me again. You are comfortable and blue.

I wear you only in the winter when it's very cold. I don't wear
you indoors. I like to put your hood on when it's very cold.

I never wear you in winter because my toes will get cold.

You are like old friends. When I put you on my feet, I feel comfortable and I can walk for miles.

Do you enjoy going out at night? Isn't it boring to be just black
and white?

Do you like it when we go swimming, or do you like it better
when we just lie on the beach?

Oh, no! There's a hole in your toe! I'll have to sew you up.

How is it possible that you have five fingers but no hand?

You have a face but no nose. You have hands but no fingers.
When I leave you home, I don't know what time it is.

I need you sometimes to hold my pants up, but usually I wear
you just because I like the way you look.

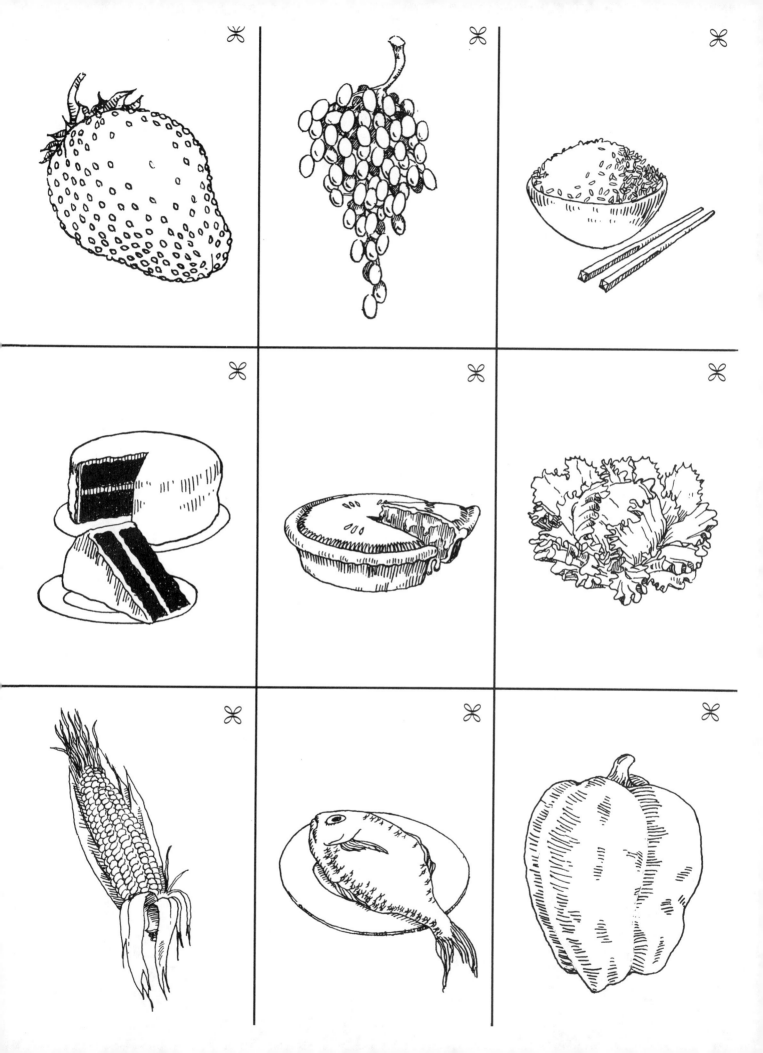

2. Food Cards
   Information Sharing
   15 minutes

What Do You Eat in Your Country?

Task: To learn how foods are prepared in different countries

Materials: One complete set of Food Cards for each group of four students.

Procedure: Divide the class into groups of four students and give each group a
            set of Food Cards. Cards should be stacked face up in the middle of
            the group. Beginning with the top card, have the first student tell the
            other three whether or not people eat that food in his or her native
            country. If the food is eaten, the student should explain how it is pre-
            pared and served. The next student discusses the next card, and so
            on until all cards are used or until time is up. After 15 minutes, ask
            the students in each group to tell the whole class what they learned
            about food in other countries.

2. Food Cards
Information Sharing
20 minutes

Learning about Foods

Task: To get information about calories, cholesterol, sodium, vitamins, and minerals for different foods.

Materials: One set of Food Cards and three Food Information Sheets A, B, and C (pp. 23 and 25) for each group of three students. Omit Coffee and Soup Cards. Pencil and paper for each student to record information.

Procedure: Divide the class into groups of three students and distribute the Food Information Sheets so that each person in the group has a different sheet—A, B, or C. Then give each group a set of Food Cards to divide evenly among themselves.

Students are responsible for finding out about the calories (sheet A), cholesterol and sodium (sheet B), and vitamins and minerals (sheet C) found in the food items on their cards. First, students should read the Food Information Sheet they have been given.

Next, students should ask other group members about the information on their sheets. (Be sure to remind them to ask questions, not simply to read the other information sheets!) Students should write down everything they learn from the other group members. After students have gotten all the information available on sheets A, B, and C, ask them to discuss their foods with other members of the group or with the whole class.

Note: This activity can be done by itself or as the first part of the Problem Solving activity ''A Healthy Diet'' (p. 31).

Food Information Sheet A

CALORIES

apple	80	lemon	20	rice	180
orange	70	onion	40	chocolate cake	280
banana	100	eggs	100	apple pie	300
bread	60	milk	160	lettuce	20
chicken	270	spaghetti	155	corn	70
steak	350	ice cream cone	250	fish	115
hamburger	350	pizza	150	green pepper	15
carrot	30	strawberries	55		
potato	150	grapes	70		

Note that all figures are for one serving. The figures are approximate and vary according to the serving size and manner of preparation. These figures are intended to be used only for comparative purposes.

(cut page here)

Food Information Sheet B

Cholesterol		**Sodium**	
chocolate cake	32 mg	rice	627 mg
apple pie	none	bread	125 mg
fruit	none	vegetables	less than 70 mg
vegetables	none	fruit	less than 10 mg
fish	50 mg	milk	120 mg
chicken	75 mg	steak	140 mg
hamburger	77 mg	chicken	133 mg
ice cream cone	50 mg	fish	135 mg
milk	33 mg	spaghetti	less than 1 mg
steak	250 mg	ice cream cone	84 mg
eggs	250 mg	pizza	456 mg
		chocolate cake	280 mg
		apple pie	355 mg
		eggs	155 mg
		hamburger	228 mg

Note that all figures are for one serving. The figures are approximate and vary according to the serving size and manner of preparation. These figures are intended to be used only for comparative purposes.

Food Information Sheet C

VITAMINS AND MINERALS

Sources of Niacin
eggs
whole grain cereal
meat
fish
poultry

Sources of protein
meat
fish
chicken
eggs
milk
cheese
bread
spaghetti

Sources of iron
beef
eggs

Sources of Vitamin C
citrus fruits
berries
leafy green vegetables
potatoes
green peppers

Sources of Vitamin B6
milk
eggs

Sources of calcium
milk
cheese
leafy green vegetables

2. Food Cards
   Opinion Sharing
   10 minutes

What Do You Like?

Task: To find a classmate who likes a particular food.

Materials: Three different Food Cards for each student.

Procedure: Give each student three Food Cards. Tell students to walk around the
               room, asking classmates if they like any of the foods depicted on the
               three cards. When they find someone who likes one of the foods,
               they will write that person's name on the card. Students should keep
               their cards hidden as they question their classmates.

Variation: Find someone who doesn't like the food on a given card. Ask the stu-
               dent to explain why he or she doesn't like that particular food.

2. Food Cards
   Opinion Sharing
   15–20 minutes

Food Tic Tac Toe

Task: To match Food Cards to descriptions on the Tic Tac Toe Game Sheets.

Materials: One Tic Tac Toe Game Sheet (p. 29) and one complete set of Food Cards for each group of three or four students.

Procedure: The object of the game is to initial four boxes in a row—horizontally, vertically, or diagonally. Divide the class into groups of three or four students and pass out the materials. To be sure that everyone understands the information on the Tic Tac Toe Game Sheet, ask the class to suggest foods that might match the descriptions on the sheet.

The dealer shuffles the cards in a deck and places them face down in the middle of the group. Player 1 picks up the top card. He or she tells the group why the card matches a description on the game sheet. If the group agrees, Player 1 keeps the card and writes his or her initials in the appropriate square. If the group disagrees, Player 1 replaces the card in the deck and Player 2 takes a turn. Play continues until someone wins. More than one person may initial a given square.

TIC TAC TOE GAME SHEET

It is not sweet.	It cannot walk.	People eat it for breakfast.	It is red.
When it is alive, it can walk.	People eat it for dinner.	It is crunchy.	It is cold.
It is sweet.	People eat it when the weather is hot.	You don't have to cook it before you eat it.	It is a liquid.
People eat it when the weather is cold.	You have to cook it before you can eat it.	It is green.	People eat it for lunch.

A Healthy Diet

Task: To distinguish between healthy and unhealthy foods.

Materials: One complete set of Food Cards and one Healthy Diet Information
             Sheet (below) for each group of three students. Also include notes
             collected in the "Learning about Foods" activity (pp. 22-25). Students
             should work in the same groups they worked in for "Learning about
             Foods."

Procedure: Ask students to review the notes they collected in "Learning about
             Foods." Then ask them to discuss the information on the Healthy Diet
             Information Sheet. Now ask students to decide which foods are
             healthy and which are unhealthy. Cards representing healthy foods
             will be placed in one stack, cards depicting unhealthy foods in an-
             other stack. All disagreements should be discussed. After students
             have finished sorting the cards, ask them to list the "good" and
             "bad" foods they usually eat. Have different groups compare lists.

(cut page here)

Healthy Diet Information Sheet

Proteins are used for the growth and repair of muscles and organs. They also give
us calories for energy.

Calcium helps our bones and teeth grow and stay strong.

Iron is important for keeping our blood healthy.

Vitamin C keeps the connecting material between cells healthy.

High-calorie foods cause weight gain.

Foods high in cholesterol increase the risk of heart problems.

Foods high in sodium increase the risk of high blood pressure or stroke.

2. Food Cards
   Problem Solving
   20 minutes

Planning a Picnic

Task: To select food for a picnic.

Materials: One complete set of Food Cards for each group of four or five
             students.

Procedure: Divide the class into groups of four or five students and give each
             group a set of Food Cards. Tell each group that they are going to
             plan a picnic and that they should choose picnic foods from their
             cards. After ten minutes, place the students in different groups and
             have them compare and explain their choices.

Variation: Each group could plan the food for a different event: a wedding, a
             party, a day at the beach, etc. Again, students should explain their
             choices.

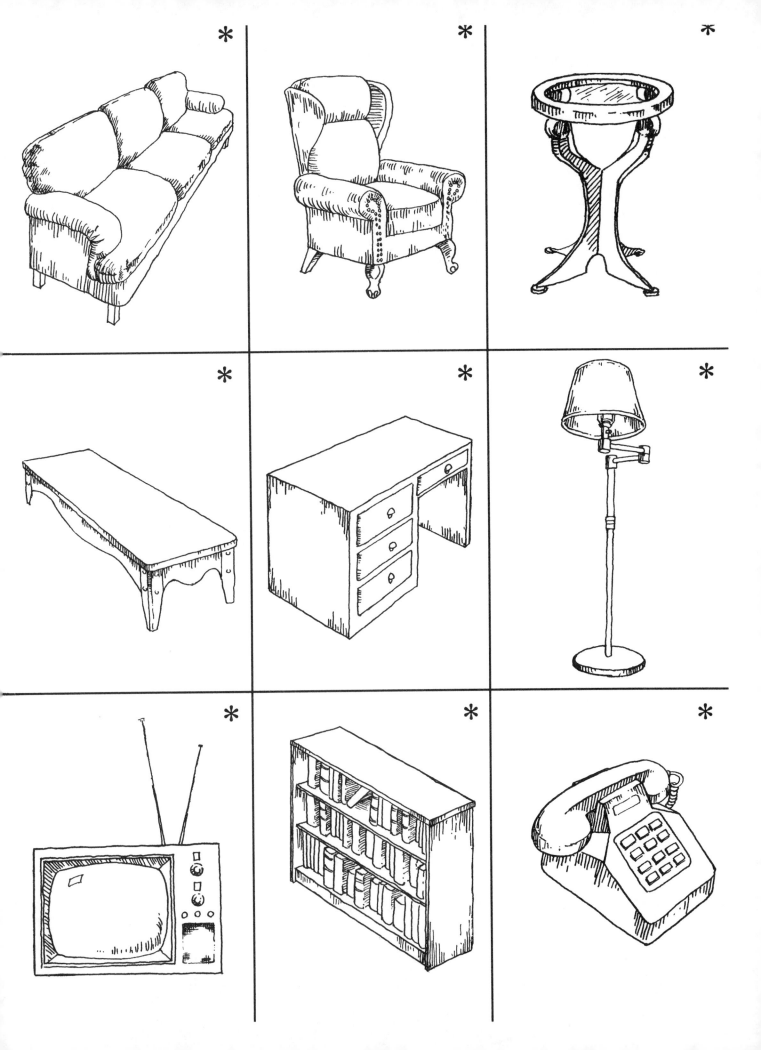

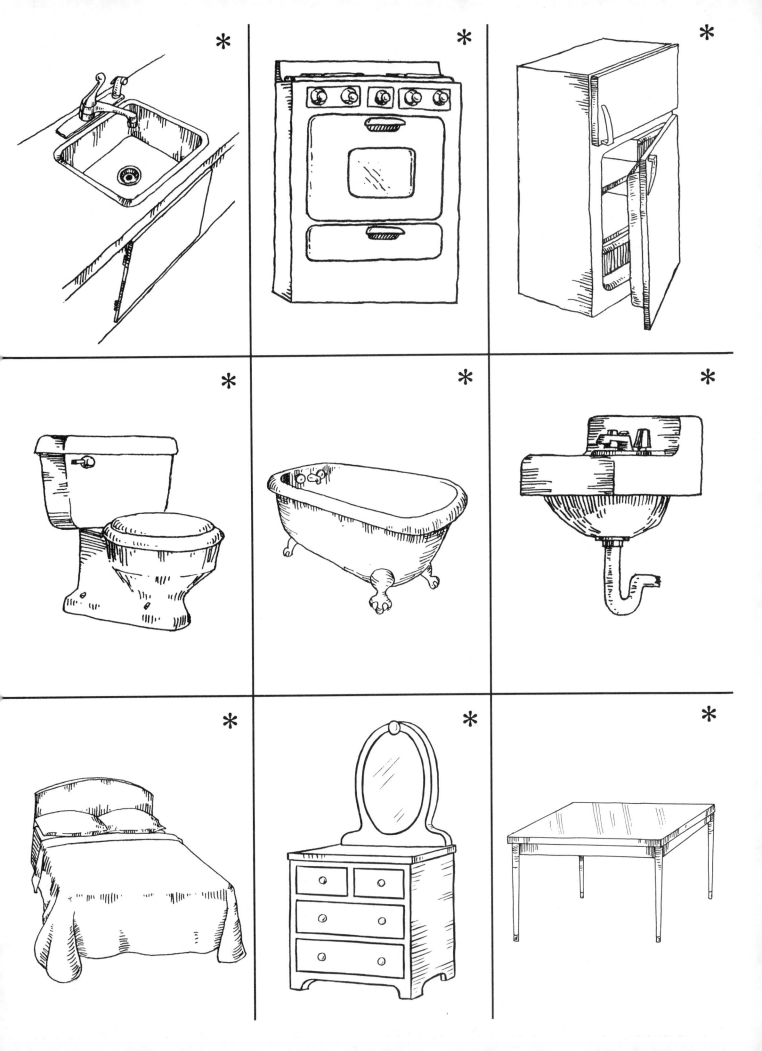

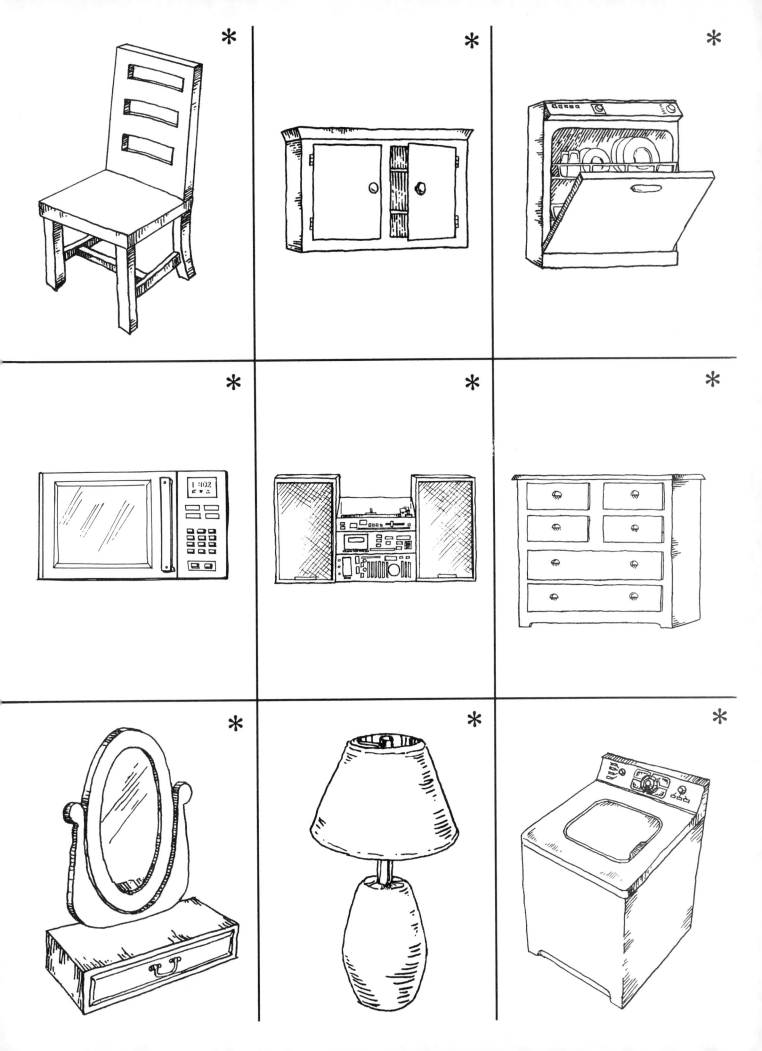

Where Is It?

Task: To describe the location of furniture on a floor plan.

Materials: A roll of tape, a large sheet of paper with a window and a door drawn on it, and eight to ten Furniture Cards depicting furniture that might be found in a living room.

Procedure: Show the whole class the sheet of paper. Tell them it is the floor plan of a living room. Locate the door and window for them. Then ask three students to leave the classroom.

Have the rest of the class arrange the Furniture Cards on the sheet of paper and tape each card in place. As they do so, have them describe where each piece is in relation to the door, to the window, and to other furniture. Then hide the sheet of paper.

Invite the first student back into the classroom. Tell the class to describe to the student where each piece of furniture is located in the living room. The student can ask questions to clarify anything he or she doesn't understand. (You may wish to allow the first student to make notes or draw a floor plan for reference.)

Invite the second student back into the room. The first student—without help from the rest of the class—will describe to the second student where each piece of furniture is located.

Finally, invite the third student back into the room and have the second student describe how the furniture is arranged. The third student repeats the description. Then show the entire class the floor plan. Have them compare the third student's account with the way the room is actually arranged. Ask the class to identify when and why errors were made.

Variation: To increase the level of difficulty, show students a floor plan with several windows and doors. Windows and doors should be different sizes or shapes so students can distinguish among them as they describe the location of furniture items.

Furniture Descriptions

Task: To match written descriptions to Furniture Cards.

Materials: Each pair of students will need the following: one copy each of the Sofa, Desk, Television set, Bed, Kitchen table, Straight chair, Cupboard, and Table lamp cards; four of any other Furniture Cards; one copy of Furniture Description Sheet A and one of Furniture Description Sheet B (p. 43).

Procedure: Cut the Furniture Description Sheet into two pieces. Then pair up the class and hand out the materials, giving Sheet A to one partner in each pair and Sheet B to the other. Ask students not to show the sheets to their partners.

Have partners place the cards face up between them. Tell students with Sheet A to read the first description on the list to their partners. Students with Sheet B then select the card that matches the description. Partners must agree on the cards selected, and disagreements should be discussed until partners can resolve them.

Next, students with Sheet B read the first description on their sheets. Their partners choose the matching card. Again, partners must agree on the cards chosen.

Students take turns reading until all of the descriptions on the sheets have been matched to Furniture Cards. Finally, put pairs of students together in groups of four to compare answers.

Follow-up: Students may write their own descriptions of the remaining Furniture Cards, writing in pairs or individually.

Furniture Description Sheet A

1. It has four legs and a horizontal top. It is sometimes made of wood. It usually has at least one drawer. People use it when they study. They use it when they do homework or write letters, pay bills or taxes.

2. Sometimes it has legs, and sometimes it is on the floor. Part of it is soft. Sometimes people study on it, but they usually feel sleepy when they do that. Some people sit on it or throw their clothes on it. Most of the time people sleep on top of it. A room is named for it.

3. It has four legs and a horizontal top. It is usually made of wood. People use it when they prepare and eat food. They use it when they play cards or other games. They also use it when they write.

4. It has four vertical legs. It is sometimes made of wood. It has a high back. On top of its legs is a horizontal piece. This is an important piece, because it is where people sit. People sit on it when they study and when they eat. It has room for only one person at a time.

(cut page here)

Furniture Description Sheet B

1. It is usually in the living room. It has very short legs. On top of them it has a long horizontal piece. It also has a long back. It is usually soft and comfortable. Two or three people can sit on it. Sometimes people take naps on it.

2. People like to look at it, but it is not really beautiful. It looks like a big box. On the front is a piece of glass and some buttons and knobs. It also has an electrical cord. When someone pushes a button, a picture appears behind the glass. The picture moves.

3. This is something in which you put things. It looks like a box with a door on it. It is attached to the wall. It is usually in the kitchen but can also be in other rooms. In the kitchen, people keep dishes, glasses, and some kinds of food in it.

4. It can be almost any shape. It usually sits on a table or desk. It has an electrical cord. It helps people see better in the dark.

It's All in a Word

Task: To match adjectives and furniture items.

Materials: A complete set of Furniture Cards and an Adjective List (below) for each group of three or four students.

Procedure: Divide the class into groups of three or four students. Give each group a set of Furniture Cards and an Adjective List. Tell students to assign the adjectives to the furniture items. Each adjective must be used at least once, and each furniture item must have at least three adjectives.

(cut page here)

ADJECTIVE LIST

imported	luxurious	shiny
comfortable	plastic	ornate
interesting	handmade	heavy
entertaining	Formica	hard
wooden	old-fashioned	cold
functional	uncomfortable	useful
oval	mass-produced	metal
rectangular	informative	short
attractive	inviting	tall
modern	electrical	boring
soft	ceramic	light
square	low	paper

Necessities

Task:
To decide which furniture items are necessities.

Materials:
One complete set of Furniture Cards for each group of three or four students.

Procedure:
Divide the class into groups of three or four students and give each one a complete set of Furniture Cards. Tell them to imagine that they are a young couple about to get married and set up housekeeping. The money they have is limited. The students are to select from their furniture cards the ten most essential items for their house. The entire group must agree on the items. After they have chosen ten, have them rank those cards in order of importance.

Next, ask the groups to do the same thing for a 23-year-old male foreign student coming to live in the United States for three years. Have the whole class discuss the results.

Variation:
A family owns all of the items shown on the Furniture Cards. Suddenly they lose all of their money and have to sell things. Have the class decide which ten items they would get rid of first.

Where Should I Put It?

Task: To examine cultural differences in home furnishing.

Materials: One complete set of Furniture Cards for each group of five or six students and one Apartment Plan (p. 49) for each member of the group.

Procedure: Divide the class into groups based on a common language, culture, or country.

Give a complete set of Furniture Cards to each group and an Apartment Plan to each person in the group. Ask the groups to review the cards and agree on which items would be found in a typical apartment in their native countries. Next, ask the groups to decide where these items would be located in the apartment plan they have been given. When they have agreed, have each group member write the names of the items on his or her Apartment Plan. If the plan does not seem suitable (other rooms are needed, for example), the group can redraw the Apartment Plan so that it resembles a typical apartment in their native countries.

Now redivide the class so that students from different groups are together. Ask them to compare their diagrams. Finally, draw the Apartment Plan on the board and discuss the findings of the whole class.

Note: It is essential to the success of this activity that students be from more than one country. The size of groups for this activity will depend upon the students' native languages and countries of origin. If possible, try to limit groups to five or six students.

APARTMENT PLAN

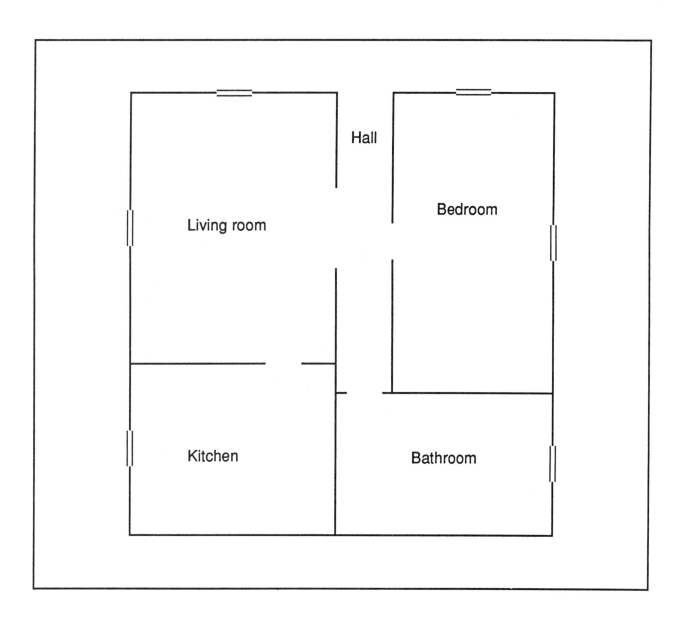

Hall

Living room

Bedroom

Kitchen

Bathroom

I Am a Chair

Task: To negotiate furniture arrangements and describe them.

Materials: A different Furniture Card for each student if there are more students
             than cards, prepare blank index cards—"wild cards"—for the addi-
             tional students. Omit any cards that might embarrass or offend
             students.

Procedure: Give each student a different Furniture Card. If there are extra stu-
             dents, give each of them one "wild card." The "wild cards" can be
             used to represent any furniture item a student wishes.

             The floor of the classroom will represent the floor plan of an apart-
             ment. The teacher may determine in advance the size and shape of
             rooms or have students decide them. Rooms should be marked off
             with chalk, chairs, or pieces of rope placed on the floor.

             The object of the activity is to have the students negotiate with each
             other over the arrangement of the furniture in the apartment. Each
             student is responsible for the item pictured on his or her card. As
             they decide on the placement of furniture items, students will stand
             in the place agreed upon for each piece of furniture. When every-
             body is in place, each student will describe his or her placement in
             relation to those nearby.

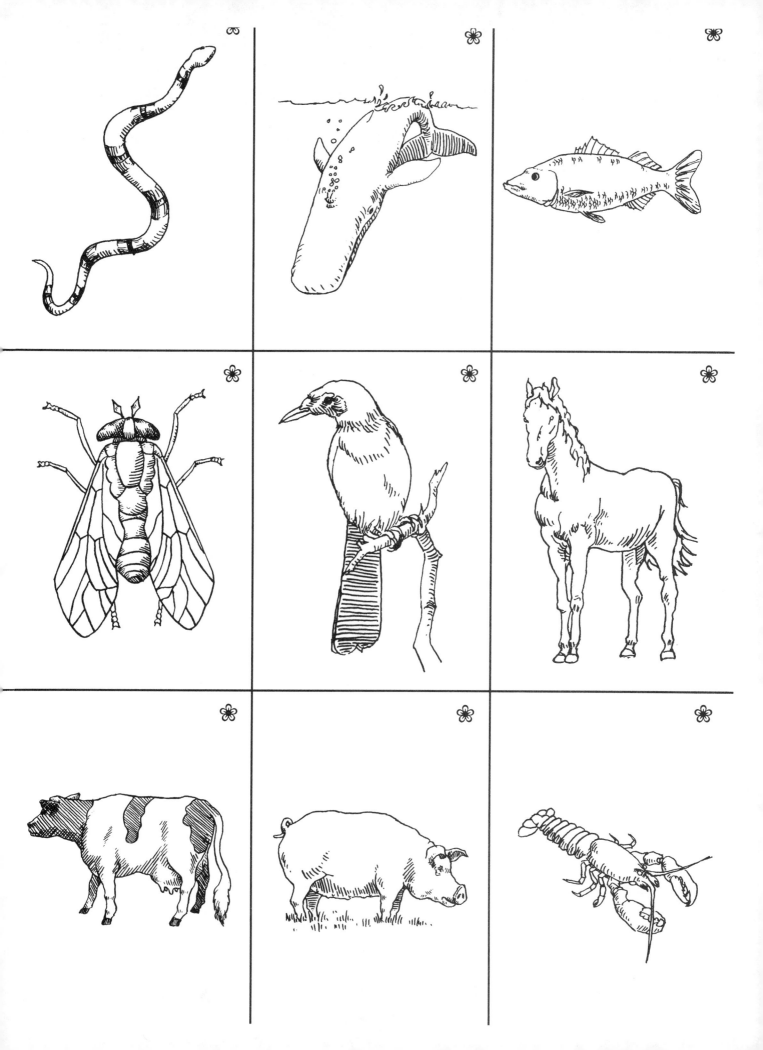

Comparisons

Task: To compare pairs of animals. The object of the game is to use adjectives to compare the animals on the cards.

Materials: One complete set of Animal Cards for each group of three to five students.

Procedure: On the board, list adjectives that could be used to describe animals (see sample list below). The adjectives can come from the teacher or be elicited from the students. After reviewing the adjectives with the whole class, divide the class into groups of three to five to begin the game.

Place a set of Animal Cards face down in the middle of each group. Player 1 picks up the top two cards. He or she places one card face up where the other players can see it but does not show the other card.

Player 1 compares the two animals on the cards using the adjectives the class has reviewed. For example, if Player 1 picks up the monkey and the owl cards, the comparisons might be: "They are both wild. They are both smart. One is furry. The other is feathered. Neither is slow nor stupid." Player 1 continues to make comparisons until someone guesses the hidden card. The player who guesses correctly chooses the next two cards. The game continues until all cards have been chosen.

SAMPLE LIST OF ADJECTIVES

small	big	dangerous	wild	beautiful
ugly	smart	stupid	fast	slow
feathered	light	friendly	tall	furry
man-eating	scaly	endangered	tasty	dirty

Which Animal?

Task: To classify animals and match classifications to Animal Cards.

Materials: One copy each of Information Sheet A (p. 61, top) for half the students in the class. One copy of Information Sheet B (p. 61, bottom) for each of the remaining students. The following Animal Cards for each pair of students: Snake, Fish, Lobster, Cat, Chicken, Turtle, Butterfly, Cockroach.

Procedure: Pair up the students. Give one partner in each pair Information Sheet A, and give Information Sheet B to the other partner. Students should not show their information sheets to their partners.

              Give each pair the cards listed above and tell the students to lay them face up on the table. Tell students they are to elicit information about animals 1–4 on Information Sheets A and B. They should first read their information sheets, then ask their partners for the information missing from each sheet.

              Students write the answers they receive on their sheets. When students have elicited all the missing information, they look at the cards and decide which animal matches the description on the information sheets.

Follow-up: Have each student choose an Animal Card that has not been described. Ask the student to classify it the way animals 1–4 were classified on the information sheets. They should consult encyclopedias and other reference texts.

Note: This activity is designed to reinforce animal classification information studied by students in biology or general science classes.

Answers: **1.** Snake   **2.** Lobster   **3.** Chicken   **4.** Cat

Animal Information Sheet A

	Animal 1	Animal 2	Animal 3	Animal 4
Classification		Arthropod	Vertebrate	
Reproduction	Lays eggs, abandons them; young look like small adults			Young develop inside mother's body; remain dependent for a few weeks after birth while she provides milk
Respiration	Lungs		Lungs	
Body Form		Segmented, hard skeleton on outside; 5 pairs of walking legs, the 1st pair of which are for holding	Bony skeleton. 2 legs, 2 wings; poor flier; scaly skin and feathers	
Food	Eats animals			Eats animals

(cut page here)

Animal Information Sheet B

	Animal 1	Animal 2	Animal 3	Animal 4
Classification	Vertebrate			Vertebrate
Reproduction		Eggs attached to female until hatched; young look very different from parents	Eggs must be kept warm until hatched; young similar to parents but smaller and have underdeveloped feathers	
Respiration		Gills for breathing underwater		Lungs
Body Form	Long, narrow; bony skeleton; no legs; scales			Bony skeleton; 4 legs; fur
Food		Plant and animal matter, living and dead	Plant matter	

Would You Like to Be an Animal?

Task: To give reasons why you would or would not like to be a particular animal.

Materials: A complete set of Animal Cards for each group of three or four students.

Procedure: Divide the class into groups of three or four students and give each group a set of Animal Cards. The cards are placed face down in the middle of the group. Students take turns picking up a card and explaining why they would or would not like to be the animal on the card.

The first student who picks a card must explain why he or she would like to be the animal shown on the card. The second student explains why he or she would not. Other members of the group decide which are the best reasons for being (or not being) a particular animal.

A Good Pet

Task: To decide which animals would make good pets.

Materials: A set of Animal Cards for each group of three students, omitting the Fish, Bird, Dog, and Cat cards and any others that might seem to be obvious pets.

Procedure: Divide the class into groups of three students and have each group choose a secretary. Hand out the Animal Cards. Ask each group to decide which six animals they think would be the best pets. The secretary writes down the group's choices. Then ask the group to narrow their choices to the three best pets and to list these in order of preference. Again, the secretary writes down the choices. Finally, put two groups together and ask them to compare their choices. Have each group explain the reasons for their choices to the class.

Animal Stories

Task: To make up a story using animals as the main characters.

Materials: Four Animal Cards for each group of three or four students. Each group is given the same four cards.

Procedure: Before beginning, ask students if they know any stories in which animals act like people. (This activity is a good follow-up to reading or hearing a fable.) Then divide the class into groups of three or four students and give each group a set of four Animal Cards.

Ask students to make up a short story with the four animals as the main characters. (You may wish to decide whether the story is set in the past, present, or future.) After the stories have been completed, assign each student a partner from a different group. Have students tell each other the stories from their groups.

Follow-up: After a group has finished telling the story, each student can write it down. Students then rejoin their groups to compare their written accounts of the story.

Design a Game

Task: To design a game using Animal Cards.

Materials: One complete set of Animal Cards for each group of three or four students, plus dice, blank paper, index cards, and felt-tip pens. Students can supply the game markers, such as coins, buttons, or pins.

Procedure: Divide the class into groups of three or four students and give each group a set of Animal Cards. Tell them they have 15 minutes to design a game using their cards.

Begin by asking students to tell you some games they already know. As students design the game, they will need to write down the game's objectives, instructions, and materials (dice, markers, etc.). Help them by suggesting ways to use the markers (as pieces for taking turns), the paper and felt-tip pens (to make a game board), the index cards (as extra game cards), etc. When the groups have finished, ask them to give their instructions and materials to another group so that group can play the game.

Variation 1:   Other sets of cards may be used for this activity.

Variation 2:   Students may design a game to practice a language function or grammatical structure they have been studying.

Describe and Draw

Task:
To describe a road sign so that another student can draw it without seeing it.

Materials:
A set of four Road Sign Cards for each of half the students in the class. A set of four different Road Sign Cards for each remaining student. All students will need paper and pencil.

Procedure:
Pair up the students. Give each partner a different set of four Road Sign Cards. Ask students not to show their cards to their partners. The students then take turns describing their cards to their partners. As one partner describes a card, the other tries to draw it based on the description. The student describing the card should not look at the drawing until it is complete.

When the drawing is finished, have both students compare it to the picture on the card. They should discuss the differences between the two pictures, pointing out as many details as they can.

Variation:
This activity could be done with any other set of cards.

Describe and Arrange

Task: To arrange a set of Road Sign Cards on a grid by following spoken instructions.

Materials: Nine Road Sign Cards and a Card Book Grid (p. 75) for each student.

Procedure: Hand out the Road Sign Cards and grids. Review the names of road signs with students if necessary. Then have the students write the following location terms on the grid: top row, middle row, and bottom row; left column, middle column, and right column.

Next, model instructions for arranging the cards: "Put the Railroad Crossing sign in the middle column of the middle row. Put the Food sign in the top row, left column." Do this several times until students know how to give instructions for arranging the cards themselves.

Now divide the students into pairs (Student A and Student B). Student A arranges the cards on his or her grid, concealing the arrangement of cards from Student B. Student A then describes the location of each card (as in the examples above) to Student B. Student B listens to the description, then tries to arrange the cards on his or her grid in exactly the same way as the cards on Student A's grid. After all nine spaces on the grid have been filled, students compare their grids. Partners then change roles and repeat the activity.

CARD BOOK GRID

5. Road Sign Cards
   Opinion Sharing
   15–20 minutes

Design a Sign

Task: To design a set of road signs.

Materials: One complete set of Road Sign Cards, manila paper, and several felt
             tip pens for each group of three or four students.

Procedure: Divide the class into groups of three or four students and give each
             group a set of Road Sign Cards. Ask students to choose the road
             signs that illustrate their messages most effectively, and also those
             that communicate least effectively. Ask students to discuss the rea-
             sons for their choices.

             Now ask students to design their own road signs, conveying the fol-
             lowing messages:

                 No eating here
                 No talking
                 Road ends
                 Library ahead
                 Elephants crossing
                 Hole in the road ahead
                 Minimum speed 20 mph
                 Next turnoff is Highway 40 to St. Louis
                 Accident ahead

             Ask the groups to add one more sign entirely of their own making.
             When groups have finished, ask each to exchange their sign with
             another group. Each group will try to guess the meaning of the other
             group's sign.

5. Road Sign Cards
   Opinion Sharing
   15–20 minutes

Which Sign?

Task: To select Road Sign Cards needed in given situations.

Materials: One complete set of Road Sign Cards and one Situation List (p. 79) for each group of four students.

Procedure: Divide the class into groups of four students. Give each group one copy of the Situation List and one set of Road Sign Cards. Ask the students to discuss the list, one situation at a time, and to select the road signs that would be most important in that situation. More than one sign may be appropriate for a given situation. The secretary records the group's choices.

Road Sign Situation List

1. You are on a summer vacation. You have driven a long time without a rest. You are hungry and thirsty.

2. You are driving on a highway in winter. It is raining, and the rain is beginning to freeze and turn to snow.

3. You are on a Sunday drive in the country, looking for ways to spend your free time.

4. You are driving an old car that has poor tires and brakes.

5. It is a foggy evening, and you cannot see ahead of you very well.

6. You have a flat tire.

7. You are almost out of gas.

8. It's getting dark on a country road. You see large shapes wandering across the road in front of your car. You're not sure what you're seeing.

9. You are going to be late arriving home, and you want to notify your family.

10. You're driving a large rented truck filled with your family's furniture. You're about to get on a highway you've never driven before.

5. Road Sign Cards
   Problem Solving
   20 minutes

Continue the Story

Task: To continue a story, using Road Sign Cards as prompts.

Materials: One set of Road Sign Cards for each group of three to five students,
             omitting the six cards used to model the activity (see below).

Procedure: To begin the activity, model it for students in the following way: Give
             six students one card each. Then supply the opening sentence for a
             story: ''I was driving to school today when . . .'' Ask the six students
             to continue the story by providing at least one sentence related to the
             road signs on their cards.

             When you have finished modeling, divide the class into groups of
             three to five students. Give each group a set of Road Sign Cards and
             place the cards face down in the middle of the group. Ask one stu-
             dent in the group to provide an opening sentence for a story. The
             next student draws a card and adds a sentence, relating the card to
             the story. The third student draws another card and adds a new sen-
             tence. The student who draws the last card concludes the story.

Your New Town

Task:

To select the road signs needed for streets in a brand new town.

Materials:

One complete set of Road Sign Cards and one New Town Map (p. 83) for each group of four or five students.

Procedure:

Divide the class into groups of four or five students. Give each group a set of Road Sign Cards and a copy of the New Town Map.

Tell students that they have been elected to the planning commission of a newly built town. Their job is to select the road signs for the streets of the town.

Unfortunately, there is a problem. Because of severe budget cuts, the town can afford only four road signs. Students must decide which road signs the town needs most and where they will be located. Working together, the students select four road signs and draw them on the town map. Each group will argue their decisions before the entire class.

NEW TOWN MAP

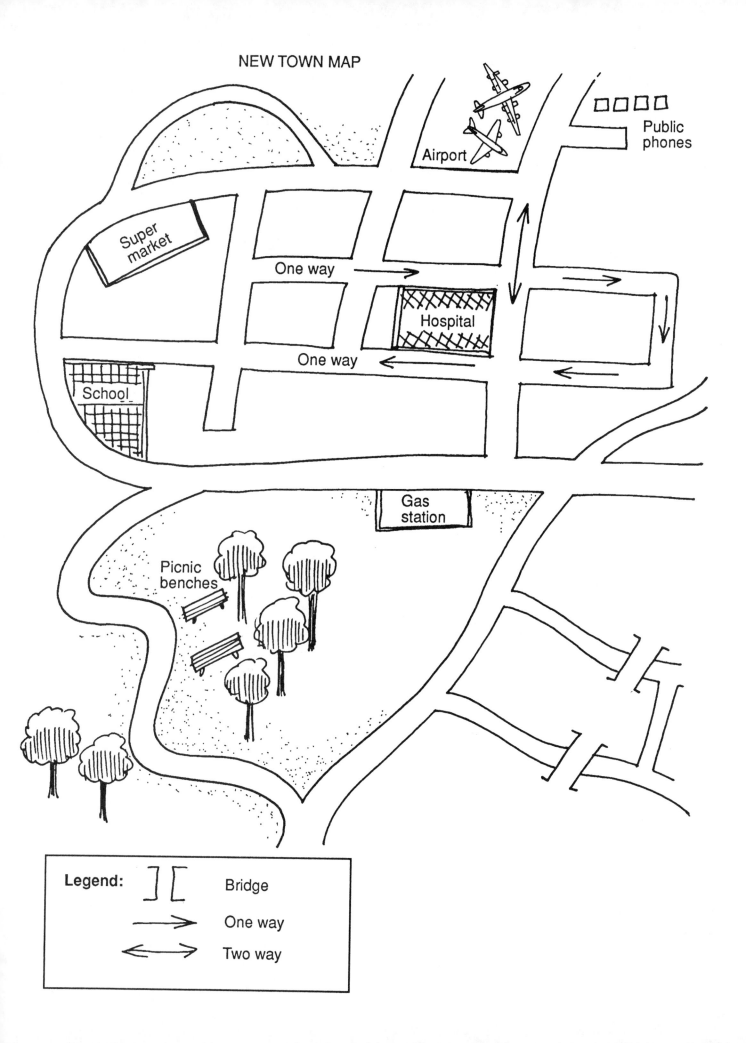

Public phones

Airport

Super market

One way

Hospital

One way

School

Gas station

Picnic benches

Legend:][Bridge

→   One way

↔   Two way

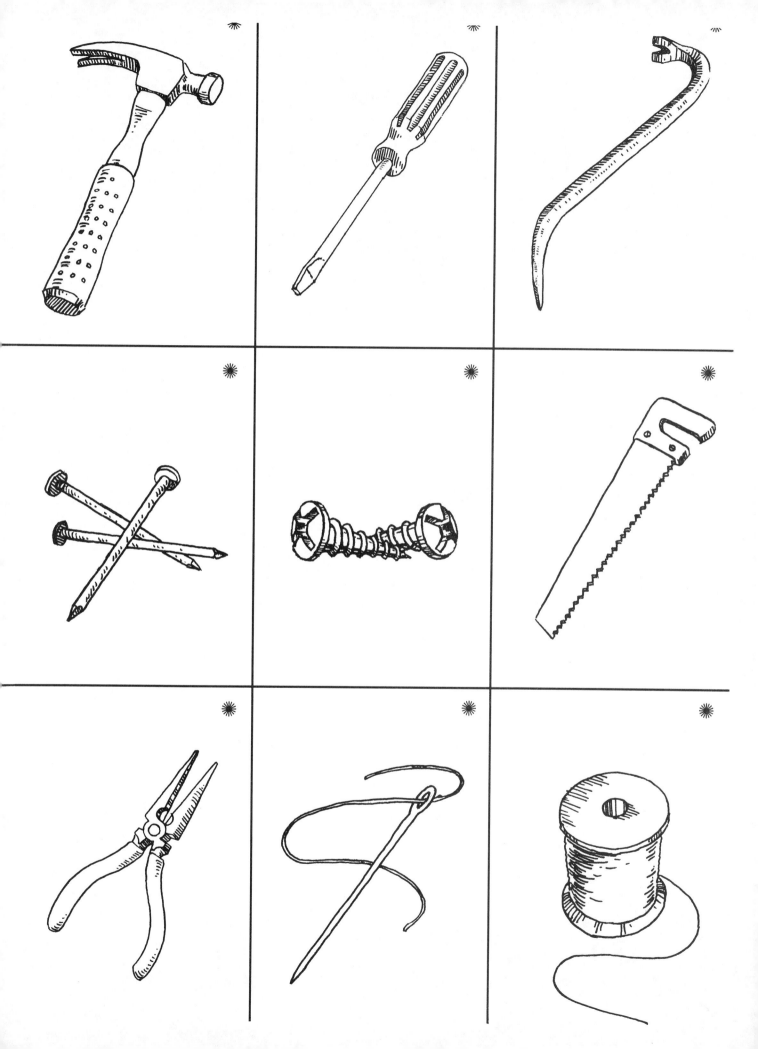

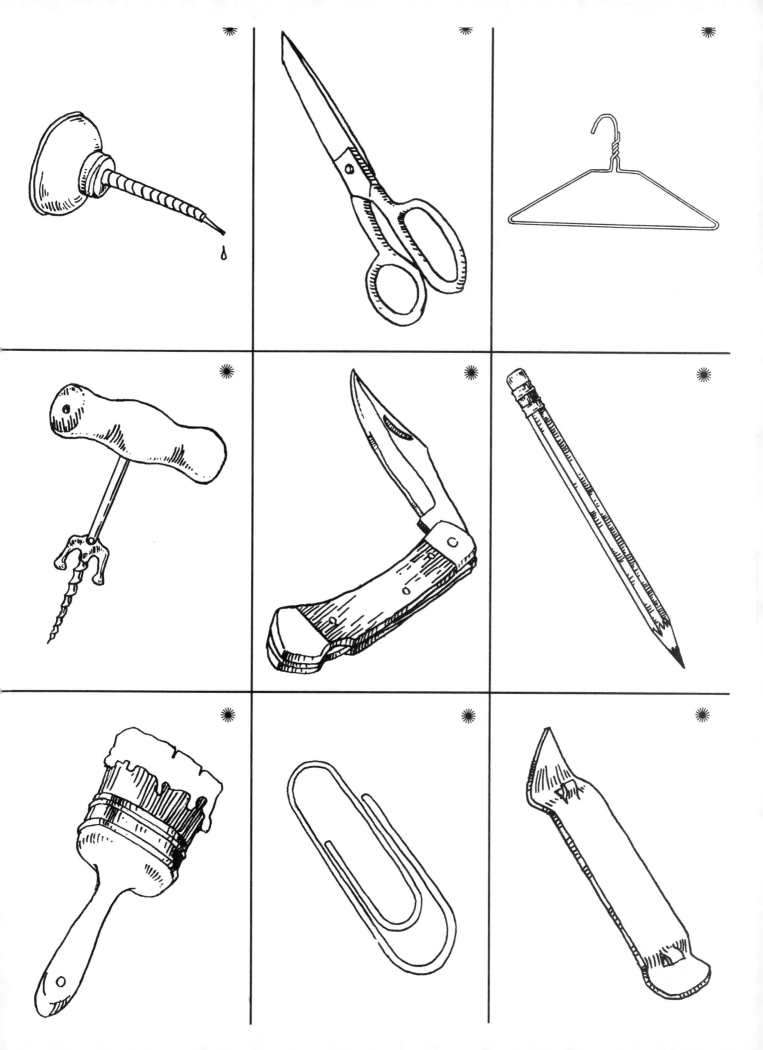

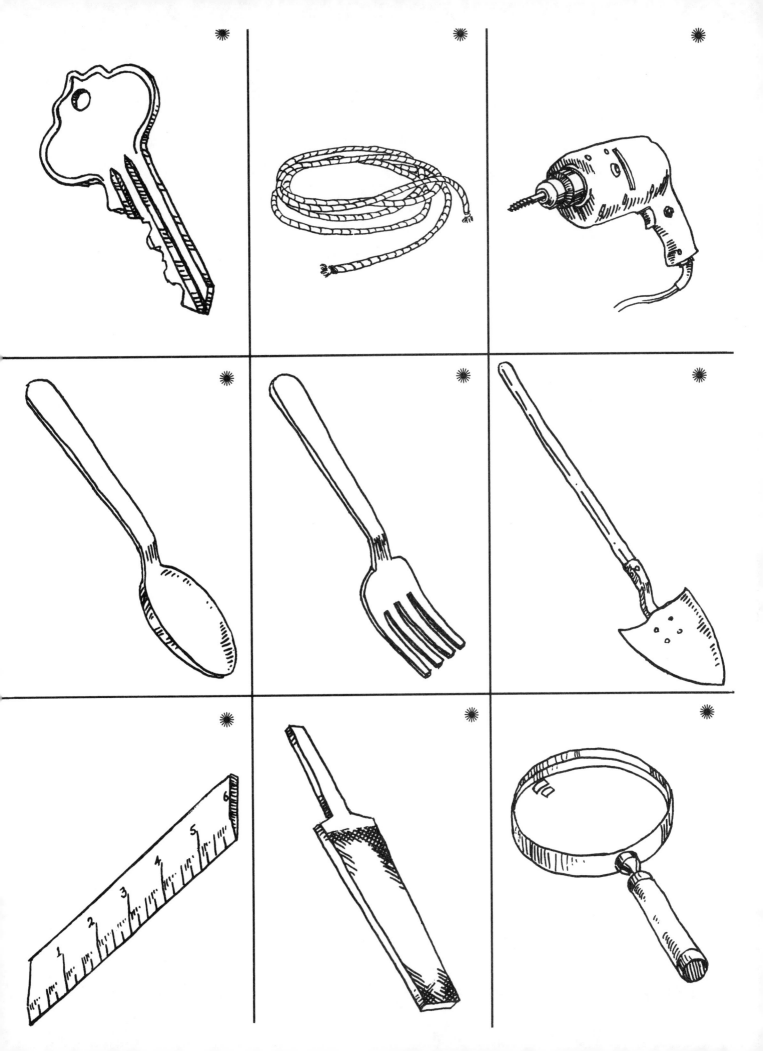

Requests

Task: To practice making requests.

Materials: Two complete sets of Tool Cards for the class. If there are fewer students than cards, omit the same cards from each set. One set should be marked in some way to differentiate it from the other. For example, print the two sets of cards on different colored paper.

Procedure: Begin by discussing ways to make requests: "May I use your . . . ?" "Do you have a . . . ?" "Could I borrow your . . . ?" Discuss ways to respond to requests positively ("Sure, here it is." "No problem.") and negatively ("I'm sorry." "I don't have one." "I'd rather not lend that.").

Give every student one card from each of the two sets of Tool Cards. Be sure that each student receives two different cards, such as a Scissors and a Coat hanger, a Hammer and an Oil can, a File and a Magnifying glass.

Explain that one card is the tool the student owns. The other card is the tool the student must borrow. The students are to walk around the classroom asking other students for the tool they need. Students must not show their cards as they make or listen to requests. The activity continues until everyone has found a matching card.

Clues Game

Task: To give clues about a hidden Tool Card. The object of the game is to guess which Tool Cards are being described by the other players.

Materials: One complete set of Tool Cards for each group of five students.

Procedure: Divide the class into groups of five students and give each group a set of Tool Cards. A dealer in each group distributes the cards evenly, setting aside extra cards. Students do not show their cards to other group members. Explain the following game instructions to the students, demonstrating with one or two cards.

Player 1 makes a statement describing a Tool Card (for example, "It is something used for sewing."). Player 1 does not say what the card is or show it to the other players. When Player 1 finishes the statement, the other players try to guess which Tool Card has been described. The other players may question Player 1 about the hidden card. If someone succeeds in guessing, Player 1 gives the card to the player who made the correct guess. If no one guesses correctly, the card is placed face up in the middle of the group, and Player 2 makes a statement about another card. The game ends when all cards have been used. The player with the most cards at the end of the game is the winner.

101 Uses

Task: To brainstorm as many uses as possible for a given tool.

Materials: One Tool Card for each student in the class. A pencil and paper for
            one student in each group of four or five students.

Procedure: Show students one Tool Card and ask them to suggest ways of using
            the tool. Encourage them to use the pattern "You can use it to . . . ";
            "You could use it to . . . "; "You might use it to . . . " More advanced
            students can be encouraged to use the passive "It can be used
            to . . ."

            Then divide the class into groups of four or five students. Give one
            Tool Card to each group member with instructions to think of as many
            uses for the tool as possible in two minutes. Each student will then
            present his or her ideas to the group. The group listens, then sug-
            gests as many additional uses as they can think of for the same tool.
            A secretary records all ideas on which the group agrees, and the
            group's list is presented to the class.

Tool Game

Task: To match Tool Cards to written descriptions.

Materials: Six Tool Cards for each student in the class. If there are not enough cards, duplicates may be used. One Tool Game Sheet (p. 95) and one die for each group of four students. Students can supply coins, buttons, pins, or other place markers for the Tool Game Sheet.

Procedure: Divide the class into groups of four students. Give each group a Tool Game Sheet, a die, and twenty-four cards. The cards are placed in a deck and held by a dealer in each group. Each student should have a marker—a coin, button, or pin.

To begin, the dealer deals six cards to each player and himself, and students place their markers on the square marked "Start." Group members take turns rolling the die and moving ahead the number of squares indicated. If a player lands on a square on which a description is written, the player must check his or her cards to see if one of them matches the description. If it does, the player puts down the card and explains to the other players why the card and description match. If the group agrees with the explanation, the player leaves the card down. If the group disagrees, the player must take back the card. If a player lands on a square with no writing, he or she waits there until the next turn.

The first player to get rid of all of his or her cards is the winner. If no one does this by the time the last player reaches the end of the board, the player with the fewest cards wins.

TOOL GAME SHEET

Finish **36**	**35**	**34**	Something to take on a camping trip **33**	Something for fixing a door **32**	**31**
25	Something for opening a bottle **26**	Something to hold two things together **27**	**28**	Something that is pointed **29**	**30**
Something for opening a can **24**	Something for hanging up clothes **23**	**22**	**21**	Something for opening a door **20**	Something for making a picture **19**
Something made of glass **13**	**14**	Something for eating **15**	Something that is sharp **16**	**17**	**18**
Something made of metal **12**	**11**	**10**	Something for sewing **9**	**8**	Something for making a hole **7**
Start **1**	**2**	**3**	Something for building a table **4**	**5**	Something that cuts **6**

Exploring Stereotypes

Task: To examine stereotypes.

Materials: One complete set of Tool Cards for each group of four students.

Procedure: Divide the class into groups of four, mixing ages, sexes, and nationalities as much as possible. Give each group a set of Tool Cards.

Ask the group to sort the cards into the following three categories:

Tools for Men   Tools for Women   Tools for Men and Women

Each group member tries to persuade the other three to agree with his or her choices. After the groups have finished, the whole class meets and compares answers.

Finally, students return to their original groups. Ask them to imagine they are living 50 years in the past. Would they still sort the tools as they did before? Would the answers change? Why? After each group has made their choices, redivide the class so that different groups may share their answers.

Help!

Task: To decide which tools would be needed in an emergency.

Materials: One complete set of Tool Cards for each group of three or four students.

Procedure: Divide the class into groups of three or four students. Assign one of the following situations to each group:

1. You fell off a boat and are stranded on a tropical island.
2. Your plane crashed in the middle of a vast desert.
3. You are lost on the side of a snowy mountain.
4. You are alone on the moon.
5. You are in prison.

Ask each group to decide which four tools would be most important to them in their situation. After each group has decided, redivide the class so that members of different groups may share their answers.

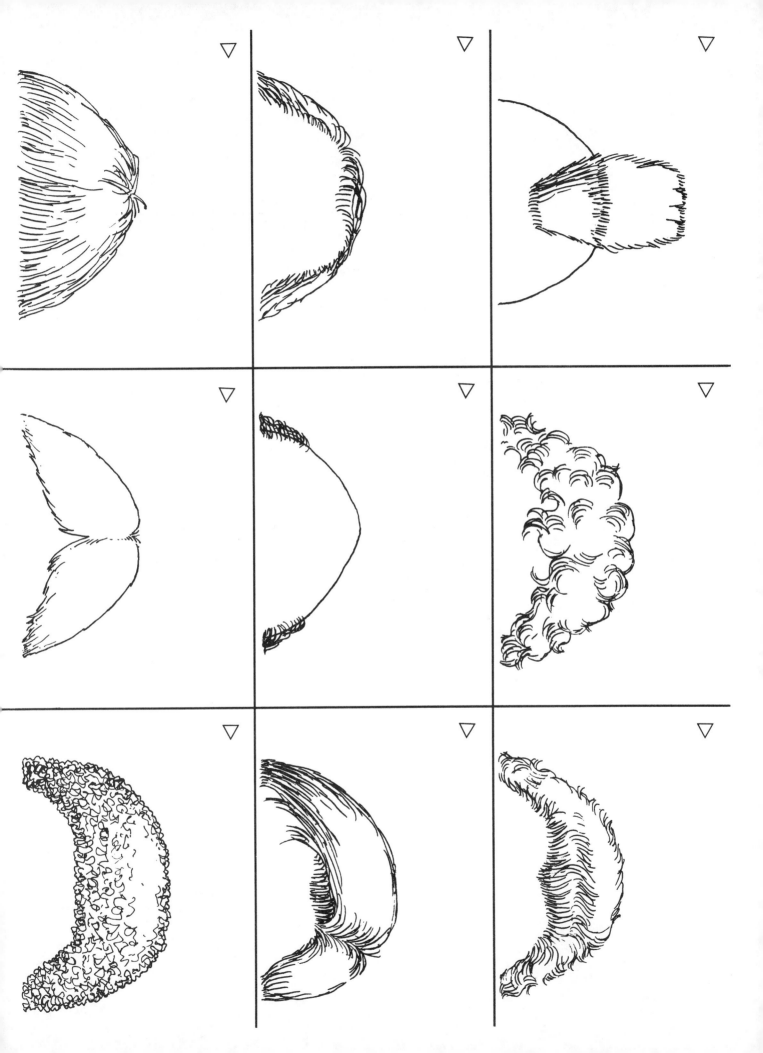

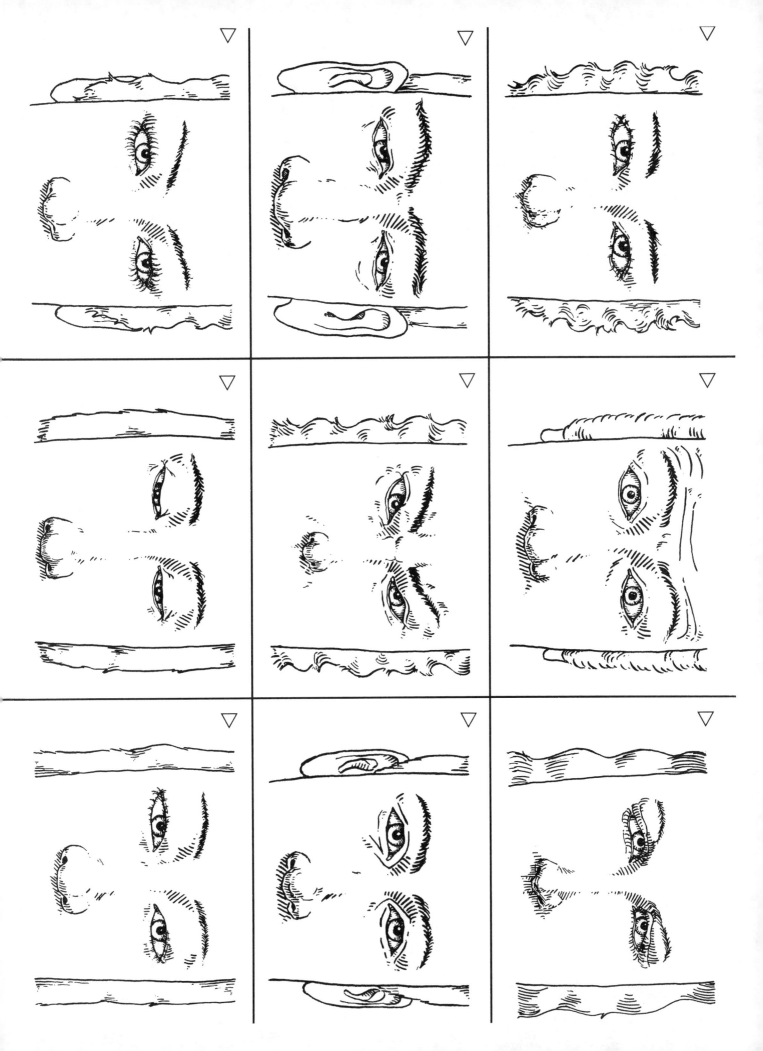

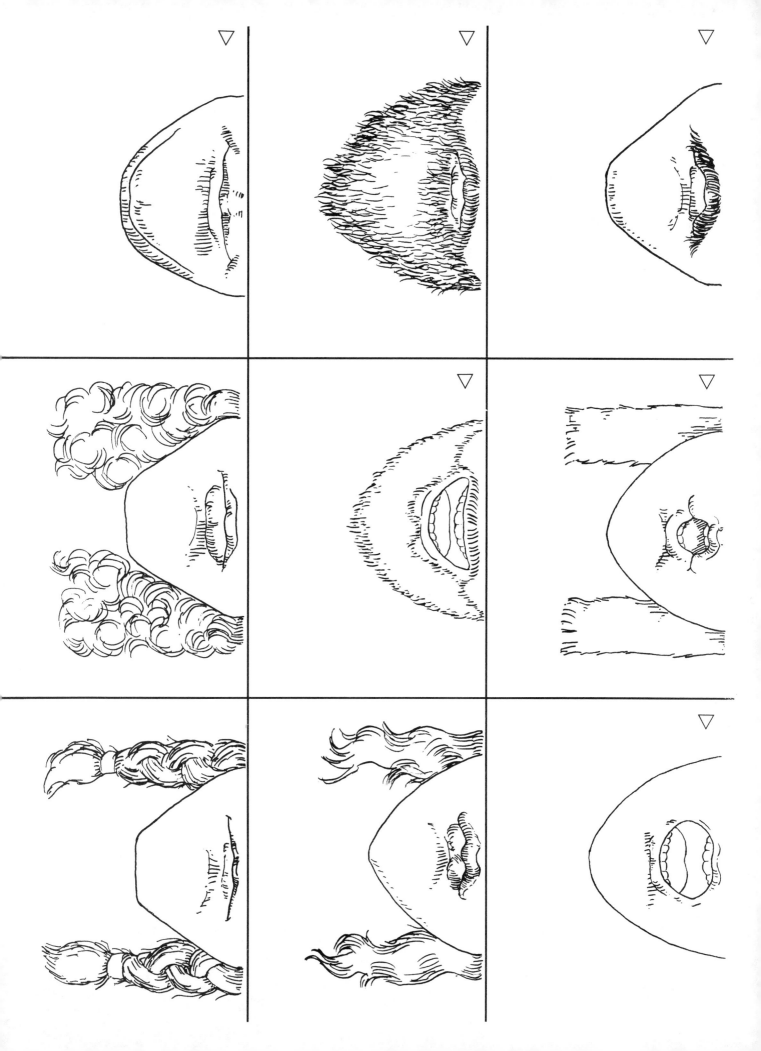

Eyewitness

Task: To describe a face so that another person can recreate it.

Materials: One complete set of Face Cards for each pair of students.

Procedure: Pair up the students in the class and give each pair a set of Face
Cards. Designate one student in each pair as the "witness" and the
other as the "detective." Tell the witness that he or she was the *only*
eyewitness to an armed robbery of a bank. The witness must describe the thief to the detective.

The witness first constructs a face out of the cards, without showing
the face to the detective. The witness then scrambles the cards and
describes the face to the detective. The detective then reconstructs
the face with the cards. As the detective is reconstructing the face,
the witness may make verbal corrections but *may not point* to any
card. When the activity is finished, players change roles and a different crime is substituted (car theft, burglary, jewel theft, etc.). A different face is constructed for each crime.

Variation 1:   The activity can also be done in groups of four, with one pair of students playing the witness and the other pair playing the detective.
The advantage to this is that students may contradict each other as
they describe the criminal, forcing the detective to ask clarification
questions.

Variation 2:   You may wish to tell students that there were two or even three crimi-
nals. Students can then construct faces for each criminal.

Changing Faces

Task: To identify changes in faces.

Materials: One complete set of Face Cards for each group of four students.

Procedure: Divide the class into groups of four students and give each group a set of Face Cards. Ask each group to use the cards to make four faces. Then ask one member of each group to leave the room. Have the remaining members change one part of each face. When they have finished, call in the students who left the room. Tell them they must identify the changes in each face by describing the part that has been changed. They must also describe the way the face looked originally. Continue the activity until each person has had a turn leaving the room.

7. Face Cards
   Opinion Sharing
   15 minutes

Reading Faces

Task: To guess what a person is thinking about.

Materials   One complete set of Face Cards for each group of four students.

Procedure: Divide the class into groups of four and give each group a set of Face
                   Cards. Instruct each student in the group to make a different face
                   with the cards. When students have completed the faces, have them
                   discuss their opinions about each face: Who is the person? What is
                   the person thinking about? What is the person feeling? Encourage
                   members of the group to ask each other questions about the different
                   faces.

7. Face Cards
   Opinion Sharing
   20 minutes

Characters

Task: To match faces and identities.

Materials: One complete set of Face Cards for each pair of students.

Procedure: Write the following identities on the board: president, movie star,
             murderer, ballerina, student, drug dealer, and teacher. (If time is a
             problem, list fewer identities.)

             Divide the class into pairs and give each pair a set of Face Cards.
             Instruct each pair to use their cards to make a face which they feel
             matches each of the identities given above. When they have com-
             pleted the task, have them change seats with a different pair. Ask
             students to try to match the faces made by the other pair to the identi-
             ties written on the board. Finally, put the two pairs together to com-
             pare their faces and choices.

Make a Story

Task: To make up a story using characters created with the cards.

Materials: One complete set of Face Cards for each group of four students. Writing paper, pencil, one or two sheets of newsprint, and a felt tip pen for each group.

Procedure: Divide the class into groups of four students and give each group a set of Face Cards. Place the cards face up in the middle of the group and ask each student to create a face from the cards. Then have students, either individually or as a group, invent a name and personality for each face. Finally, ask the group to write a short story in which all four characters appear.

             Ask each group to copy its story onto the large sheet of paper. Alternatively, have the students write the stories on overhead transparencies or have the pages xeroxed or mimeographed for the following day. When the stories have been copied, share them with the entire class.

It's All in the Face

Task: To prepare and answer questions about faces.

Materials: One complete set of Face Cards for each group of three or four students.

Procedure: Divide the class into groups of three or four students and give each group a set of Face Cards. Ask groups to put together the single most interesting face they can, working as quickly as possible. When they have done this, ask them to make up a list of ten questions about the person they have created. These might include questions about the person's age, education, hobbies, employment, love life, family, criminal record, military record, and so forth. Then ask them to exchange the face and their questions with another group, and answer the other group's questions.

Follow-up: The students can write a resume for the person they have created.

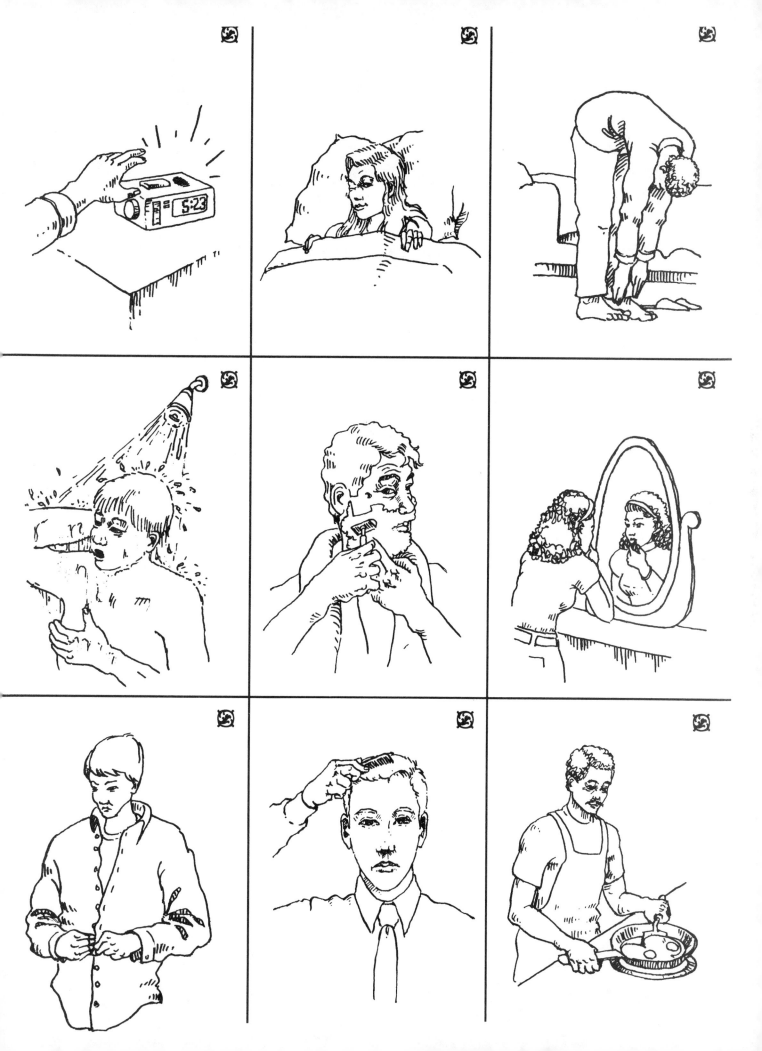

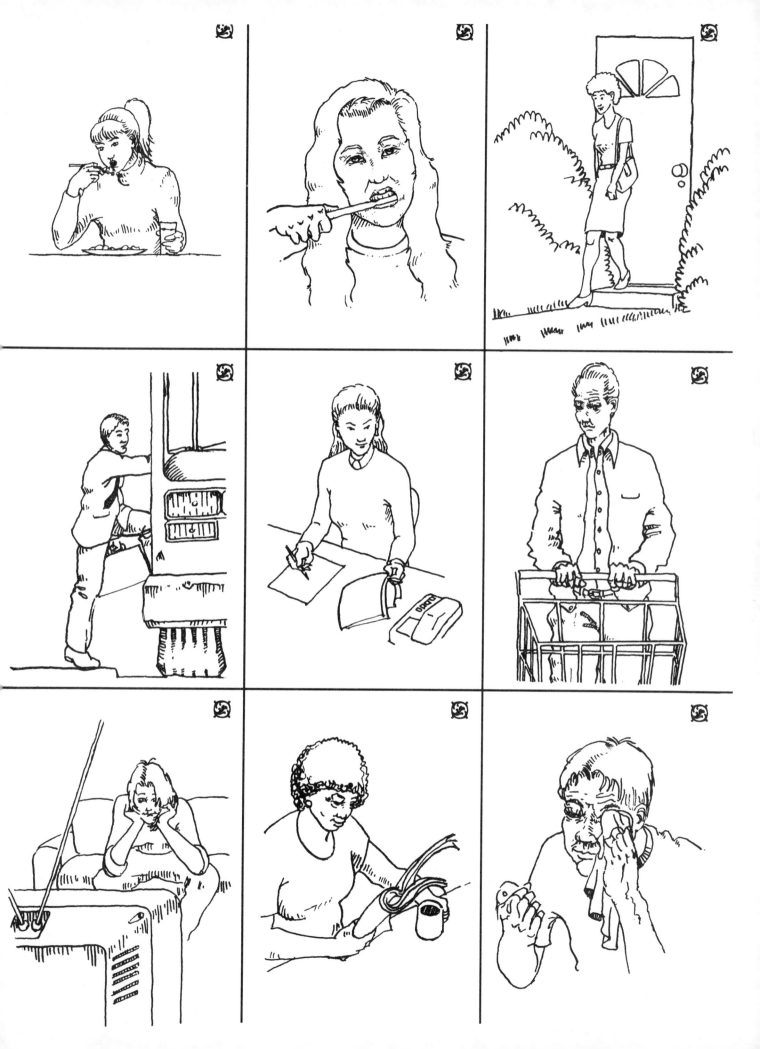

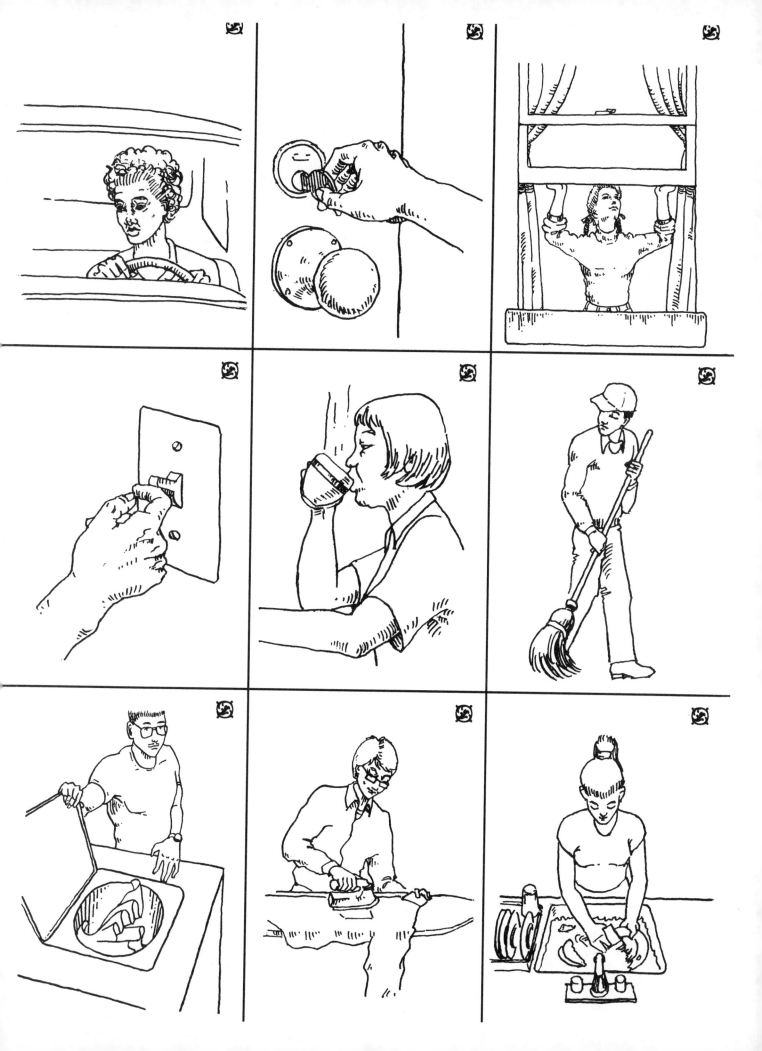

Guess the Activity

Task: To guess daily activities described by other students.

Materials: One Daily Activity Card, paper, and pencil for each student.

Procedure: Pass out the Daily Activity Cards, one for each student. Ask students not to show their cards to anyone else. Ask them to think about how they might describe, step by step, the activity depicted on their cards without naming that activity.

The teacher can help by modeling a description for the students. Taking the Comb Hair card, for example, the teacher might say: ''I pick up something. I stand in front of a mirror. I put the object in my hair. I pull it. I do it again. And again. Sometimes it hurts! As I do it, I watch myself in the mirror.'' (Be sure to remind students *not to use their hands* as they describe their activity.)

Give students a few minutes to plan what they want to say. Walk around the room, providing help as needed. After giving students time to plan, divide the class into groups of five.

Group members then take turns describing their activities. If a student cannot understand the description of an activity, he or she should ask for clarification. As each student describes an activity, other group members write down the student's name and the name of the activity being described. After everyone has had a turn, group members compare what they wrote down. As a follow-up, each group can choose the best activity description and present it to the entire class.

A Survey

Task: To survey classmates about daily activities.

Materials: One Daily Activity Card for each student.

Procedure: Give each student a Daily Activity Card. On the back of it have them write: never, less than once a day, once a day, two or more times a day. Tell them they are going to make a survey of their classmates' daily activities. Ask students to walk around the room asking each member of the class how often he or she performs the activity on the card. As they ask, they should keep track of the answers on the backs of their cards.

While students are asking their questions, the teacher writes the following headings on the board:

Never   Less than once a day   Once a day   Two or more times a day

After students have completed their survey, have them list their findings under the headings on the board. Discuss the findings with the students. How would answers be different if students had asked the same questions of their parents, grandparents, children, husbands, or wives?

Note: This activity can be related to the students' knowledge of mathematics by having them convert the numbers to percentages.

Which Ones Belong Together?

Task: To classify daily activities.

Materials: One set of Daily Activity Cards for each group of three students.

Procedure: Write the following words on the board: *a ticket, a dollar, a banana, a Coke, a plant, a pair of glasses, a light bulb, a shirt*. Ask students to think of ways they might classify these and explain their classifications. Then tell them that they are going to do the same thing with the Daily Activity Cards.

Divide the class into groups of three students. Give each group a set of Daily Activity Cards. Ask students to classify the cards into three to five categories, and to explain their criteria for classification. Give each group ten minutes to complete the task.

Then put two groups together. Ask each to examine the other's categories and guess the criteria the other group used for classifying cards.

8. Daily Activity Cards
   Opinion Sharing
   10–15 minutes

Describe It

Task: To match daily activities and adjectives.

Materials: One complete set of Daily Activity Cards, one Describe It Word Sheet (p. 121), and one die for each group of three or four students.

Procedure: Divide the class into groups of three or four students. Give each group a set of Daily Activity Cards, a Describe It Word Sheet, and a die. The dealer distributes the cards evenly, setting aside all leftover cards. Students roll the die to determine the order of play.

Player 1 rolls the die and locates the matching square on the Describe It Word Sheet. If the player rolls a 3, for example, then the matching square on the Word Sheet is square #3.

The player then selects a Daily Activity Card that can be described by the adjective in the Word Sheet square. For example, the adjective in square #3 is "interesting." The player must therefore choose a daily activity that can be described as "interesting." The player then explains his or her choice to the others in the group.

If the group agrees, the player puts down the card and rolls again. If the group disagrees, the player must either persuade them to change their minds, select another card to match the adjective, or forfeit the turn. The first player to lay down all cards is the winner.

DESCRIBE IT WORD SHEET

1 Fun	**2** Boring	**3** Interesting
4 Easy	**5** Hard	**6** Unnecessary

Before and After

Task: To arrange Daily Activity Cards in a sequence.

Materials: One of the following Daily Activity Cards for each student: Turn Off Alarm, Wake Up, Exercise, Take a Shower, Shave, Get Dressed, Comb Hair, Cook, Eat, Brush Teeth, Leave House.

Procedure: Divide the class into groups of ten. Give each student in each group a different Daily Activity Card. If there are extra students, they may be paired with others holding the same card or they may serve as "checkers," making sure that others in their group are doing the activity correctly.

Tell the students you are going to read ten sentences about the activities on their cards. Students must listen to the sentences, agree on the sequence of activities, and arrange themselves in a line that corresponds to the correct sequence.

As you read, pause so that the students can decide among themselves in which order to stand. At the end of the activity, have groups compare their results by telling the class the exact sequence in which the activities occurred.

SENTENCES

1. I eat my breakfast as soon as it's cooked.
2. I comb my hair right after I take a shower.
3. I take a shower right after I exercise.
4. As soon as I finish brushing my teeth, I leave the house.
5. I don't get dressed until just after I shave.
6. I shave right after I comb my hair.
7. I wake up at 6:00 in the morning.
8. I brush my teeth right after I eat breakfast.
9. Just after I get dressed, I cook a hot breakfast.
10. The first thing I do after I wake up is exercise.

Variation: Divide the class into pairs and give each pair the same cards as above. Then read the sentences and have students arrange the cards as you read. Read all sentences at least twice. Allow time between readings for students to discuss the arrangement of activities. Check answers by having students read their sequences. Finally, students can practice making their own "before and after" statements with the cards.

Answers: **1.** Wake up   **2.** Exercise   **3.** Shower   **4.** Comb hair
5. Shave   **6.** Get dressed   **7.** Cook   **8.** Eat
9. Brush teeth   **10.** Leave house.

Daily Schedule

Task: To make up daily schedules.

Materials: One complete set of Daily Activity Cards and one Personality Sheet
                (p. 125) for each pair of students.

Procedure: Pair up the students and distribute the Daily Activity Cards and the
                Personality Sheets. Ask the students to select any one person from
                the sheet. They will then go through their cards, keeping those cards
                they think apply to that person and setting aside those that do not.

                Next, have students decide the order in which the activities probably
                occur in the person's typical day. Finally, have them write down on a
                piece of paper the time and duration of each activity.

Variation 1:   The class can select two people and compare their daily schedules.
                This increases the time needed to perform the activity.

Variation 2:   The class can make up a list of nine famous people and decide on
                the daily activities of one or two of them.

PERSONALITY SHEET

Woman 20 years old France Student	Man 30 years old Turkey Banker	Girl 12 years old Nigeria Student
Man 43 years old Japan Artist	Woman 27 years old Venezuela Engineer	Man 19 years old England Auto mechanic
Boy 10 years old Saudi Arabia Student	Man 65 years old United States Retired	Woman 35 years old India Doctor

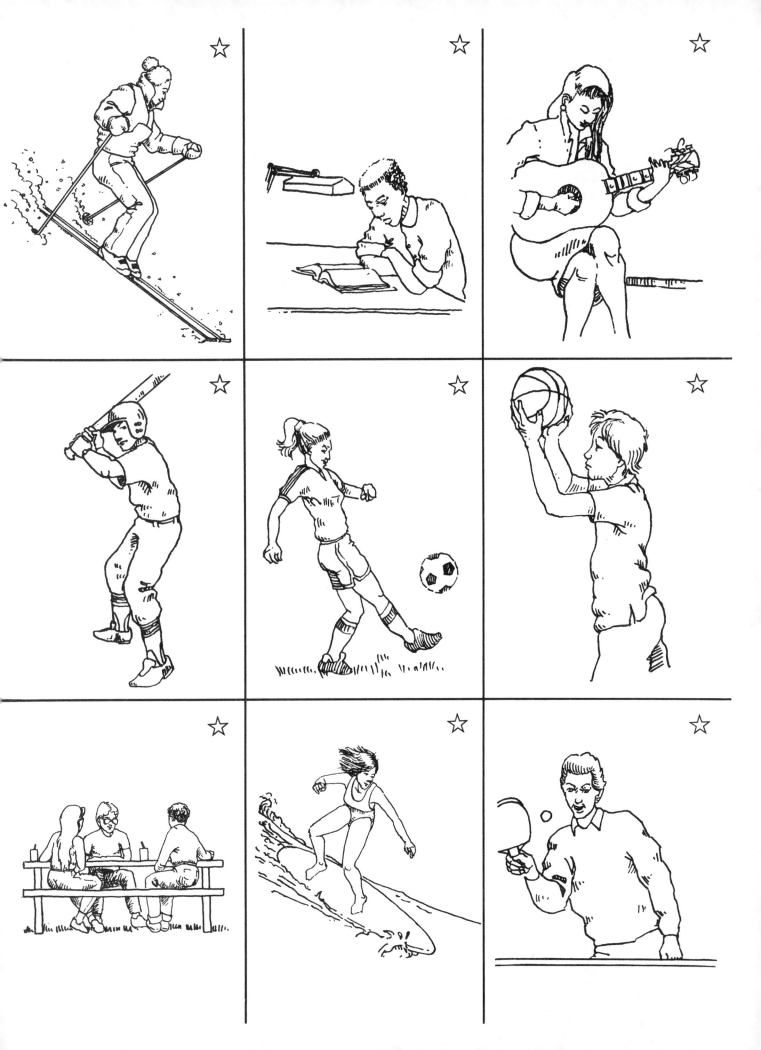

I Like to . . .

Task: To explain favorite leisure activities.

Materials: Three or four complete sets of Leisure Activity Cards, depending on
             the size of the class.

Procedure: Put all the Leisure Activity Cards face up on a desk or table. Ask stu-
             dents to take a card representing a favorite activity. Then have stu-
             dents choose partners. Students should tell their partners how to per-
             form the activity, why they like doing it, and how they became
             interested in it. Partners should ask questions and tell the speaker
             what they like or dislike about the activity. Give students three min-
             utes to talk about their activities. Then have students reverse the
             roles of teller and listener, again keeping to a three-minute time limit.

             Next ask students to find a new partner and repeat the process. This
             time allow only two minutes for presentations. Finally, have students
             change partners again, allowing only one minute for presentations.
             Ask the class to share what they found out about their classmates.

Follow-up: Ask each student to write about one classmate's favorite activity.

Pantomime

Task:
To ask yes/no questions to guess which leisure activities are being pantomimed.

Materials:
One Leisure Activity Card per student.

Procedure:
First, review yes/no questions with the students. Then select one Leisure Activity Card and pantomime the activity depicted on the card. Have students ask yes/no questions to guess what you are doing, as in the following example:

> (Teacher pantomiming climbing a mountain)
>
> Student 1: "Are you running?"
> Teacher: shakes head no.
> Student 2: "Are you riding a bicycle?"
> Teacher: shakes head no.
> Student 1: "Are you climbing something?"
> Teacher: nods head yes.
> Student 3: "Is it a ladder?"
> Teacher: shakes head no.
> (etc.)

Put all the cards in a bag and have each student take one. Ask students not to show their cards to each other. Arrange the chairs in a circle so that students can see one another. Give students a moment to think about how to act out the activity, then have them take turns pantomiming the activities on their cards. The rest of the class asks yes/no questions to guess the activity.

Variation:
In a large class, students can work in groups of six to eight. Each student can act out more than one card.

9. Leisure Activity Cards
   Opinion Sharing
   15–20 minutes

Two at Once

Task: To identify activities that can be carried out at the same time.

Materials: A complete set of Leisure Activity Cards for each group of three or four students.

Procedure: Divide the class into groups of three or four students and give each group a set of Leisure Activity Cards. Ask students to identify pairs of activities that can be done at the same time, for example, Have a Picnic and Talk with Friends, or Sit on a Beach and Paint a Picture.

After ten minutes, each pair reports on their choices. The rest of the class listens and decides if a choice is acceptable. The pair with the most acceptable choices is the winner.

Weather Game

Task: To decide which leisure activities can be performed under which weather conditions.

Materials: One complete set of Leisure Activity Cards, one copy of the Weather Game Board, and one die for each group of four players. Students can supply coins, buttons, or pins to use as markers.

Procedure: Divide the class into groups of four students. Hand out the materials. The Leisure Activity Cards should be placed face down in the middle of the board. Before beginning the game, be sure that all players understand all the weather symbols on the Weather Game Board.

All players begin at "Start." Each player in turn will roll the die and move ahead the number of squares indicated. Player 1 draws a card from the pack and states whether he or she can carry on that activity in the weather conditions shown on the square. He may say, for example, "I can swim when it's sunny" or "I can't ski when it's 100°."

If the player *can* do the activity, he or she moves ahead two squares. If the player *cannot*, he or she must move back two squares. If at least two of the other three players disagree with the player's statement, he or she must go back **four** squares. The first player to circle the board is the winner.

WEATHER GAME BOARD

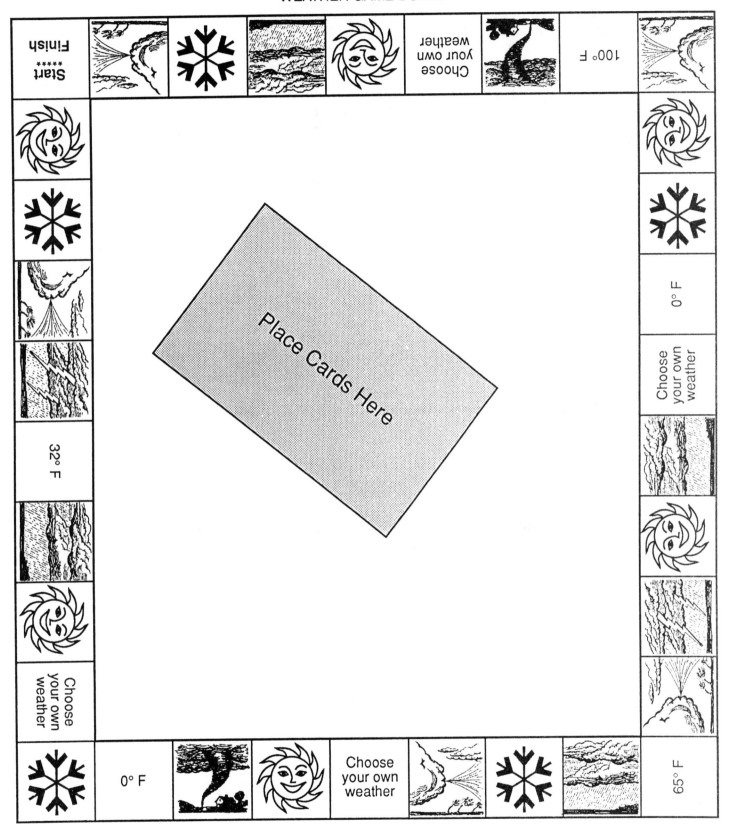

Where in the World?

Task: To choose geographical locations for different leisure activities.

Materials: A complete set of Leisure Activity Cards for each group of four stu-
               dents. A world map is optional.

Procedure: Divide the class into groups of three or four students. If possible,
               each group should be made up of people from different parts of the
               world. Hand out the Leisure Activity Cards. The first student in each
               group will draw a card and choose a place in the world where that
               activity could be done. For example, ''We could go skiing in Chile.''
               The rest of the group has to agree or disagree. If a group member
               disagrees, that person should suggest an alternative. Group mem-
               bers continue taking turns until all of the cards have been discussed.
               The activity can be shortened by using fewer cards.

Note: This activity assumes a basic knowledge of geography.
               If a map is used, students can indicate where on the map the country
               under discussion is located.

Weekend Plans

Task: To agree on weekend activities.

Materials: Nine Leisure Activity Cards for each pair of students.

Procedure: Divide the class into pairs and give each pair nine Leisure Activity Cards. Ask each pair to agree on three activities they would like to do on the weekend. Then have each pair join another pair using nine different cards. Have both pairs agree on three activities they would like to do on the weekend. Finally, ask the students to agree on one activity. Each group can report to the class on their choice.

APPENDIX A

Language for Interaction

Eliciting Information
Could you tell me . . . ?
I need to know . . .
Yes/no questions

I'd like to know . . .
Do you know . . . ?
Wh- questions

Agreeing or Disagreeing with Statements of Fact
You're right/wrong.
That's not right.
I think you're wrong.

That's true . . .
I don't think that's so.
I can/can't believe that . . .

Eliciting Opinions
What do you think about . . . ?
What's your opinion?
What's your view?

Do you think . . . ?
How do you see it?
How do you feel about . . . ?

Giving Opinions
I think . . .
I believe . . .
It seems to me that . . .

I feel . . .
In my opinion . . .

Agreeing or Disagreeing with Opinions
I agree/disagree.
I think so too.
I don't think so.

Do you really think that . . . ?
I believe you're right.
Yes, but . . .

Making Suggestions
Why not . . . ?
Let's . . .
Maybe you could . . .

We/you could . . .
Why don't you . . . ?
I have an idea.

Accepting or Rejecting Suggestions
Let's not.
No, let's . . . instead.
That's okay with me.

I don't think we should.
That's a great idea.
It sounds good to me.

Giving Reasons and Results
because/because of
as a result/as a result of
therefore

since
consequently
so that

Seeking Confirmation or Agreement
I think . . . , don't you?
Don't you agree that . . . ?

Don't you think that . . . ?

Checking Information

I'm not sure I understand . . .
Are you sure?
Do you mean . . . ?
I don't understand . . .
"What" substitution (It's a what? You did what?)

Did you say . . . ?
Are you certain?
It's not clear to me . . .
Let me get this straight . . .

Asking for Clarification

Can you explain more about . . . ?
Are you saying . . . ?

What do you mean by . . . ?
Could you tell me more about . . . ?

Asking for Repetition

Could you repeat that?
Could you say that again?
Huh?
Sorry, I didn't get that.
I didn't understand.

What was that?
Would you mind repeating that?
Pardon me?
Excuse me?
I didn't catch what you said.

Checking Instructions

Are we supposed to . . . ?
Do you want us to . . . ?
Should we . . . ?

Did you tell us to . . . ?
Am I supposed to . . . ?
So you want me to . . . ?

Taking Turns

Excuse me.
I'd like to say that . . .
May I say something here?
I think . . . , don't you?
What do you think?

Can I just add . . . ?
Could I ask a question?
What do you think?
Don't you agree/think that . . . ?
Let's hear your ideas.

APPENDIX B

Activities Arranged by Function

Expressing Probability

Guessing

Giving Instructions

Requesting

Making, Refusing, Accepting Offers

Expressing Likes, Dislikes, Preferences

APPENDIX C

Activities Arranged by Grammatical Structure

APPENDIX D

Life Skills

Clothing: identification, colors, sizes, parts of clothing (sleeves, collars), prices, shopping, budgeting, appropriateness, advertising, returns

Food: identification, colors, forms, meals, times, diet and health, shopping, selection, preparation, appropriateness, cultural differences

Furniture: identification and purpose, shopping, budgeting, housing, floor plans, repairs, cultural differences, prioritizing

Animals: identification and classification, pets, fables

Road Signs: identification and function, driving tests, travel, safety

Tools: identification and function, workplace, housing, repairs

Faces: identification of facial features, descriptions of people, expressions, interpretations, resume writing, life history

Daily Activities: identification, time, days of the week, sequencing, surveying, rating activities, daily schedules

Leisure Activities: identification, weather, seasons, months, rating activities, personal interests, geography, making plans